Android
Tablets
Explained
For All Ages

Jim Gatenby

BERNARD BABANI (publishing) LTD
The Grampians
Shepherds Bush Road
London W6 7NF
England

www.babanibooks.com

D0522308

Please Note

Although every care has been taken with the production of this book to ensure that all information is correct at the time of writing and that any projects, designs, modifications and/or programs, etc., contained herewith, operate in a correct and safe manner and also that any components specified are normally available in Great Britain, the Publishers and Author do not accept responsibility in any way for the failure (including fault in design) of any project, design, modification or program to work correctly or to cause damage to any equipment that it may be connected to or used in conjunction with, or in respect of any other damage or injury that may be so caused, nor do the Publishers accept responsibility in any way for the failure to obtain specified components.

Notice is also given that if equipment that is still under warranty is modified in any way or used or connected with home-built equipment then that warranty may be void.

First Published – April 2014

British Library Cataloguing in Publication Data:

A catalogue record for this book is available from the British Library

ISBN 978-0-85934-749-5

Cover Design by Gregor Arthur

Printed and bound in Great Britain for Bernard Babani (publishing) Ltd

About This Book

The Android operating system (OS) software controls most of the world's tablet computers and smartphones. Some manufacturers modify Android to suit their own needs but even these "tweaked" versions still have much in common with the standard Android.

This book has been prepared using several of the top-selling Android tablets. These included standard Androids and also the "tweaked" Samsung Galaxy Tab 3 with the TouchWiz interface. TouchWiz is a "front end", installed on top of the Android OS on the range of Samsung Galaxy tablets and smartphones. Although TouchWiz has a different "look and feel" from standard Android, the basic features and icons are the same or similar. Where there are differences these are explained in the text.

The first chapter gives an overview of the Android family and the essential technical terms, followed by setting up a new tablet, connecting to the Internet and creating a Google account. Exploring the various screens and personalising them is then covered, including downloading and installing apps (or software) from the Google Play Store. How to do this for the Kindle Fire HD/HDX ("sideloading") is beyond the scope of this book.

Later chapters describe browsing the Web, with searches using text and voice input. Reading eBooks using Google and Kindle apps is then discussed, followed by YouTube, music, video and live and catchup television. Social networking, e-mail, Skype, Facebook and Twitter are also covered.

Chapter 8 describes the use of the "clouds" on the Internet to store photos and documents, accessible from any computer. Also using free software from the clouds, including the Google Docs word processor and spreadsheet and Google Cloud Print.

Managing your Android by connecting it to a PC or using a file manager app is discussed, together with connecting external devices such as flash drives, SD cards and Micro SD cards. Also connecting your tablet to an HDMI TV, monitor or projector. The cameras built into most Androids are also described.

About the Author

Jim Gatenby trained as a Chartered Mechanical Engineer and initially worked at Rolls-Royce Ltd using computers in the analysis of jet engine performance. He obtained a Master of Philosophy degree in Mathematical Education by research at Loughborough University of Technology and taught mathematics and computing in school for many years before becoming a full-time author. His most recent teaching posts included Head of Computer Studies and Information Technology Coordinator. The author has written over forty books in the fields of educational computing and Microsoft Windows, including many of the titles in the highly successful "Older Generation" series from Bernard Babani (publishing) Ltd.

The author has considerable experience of teaching students of all ages and abilities, in school and in adult education. For several years he successfully taught the well-established CLAIT course and also GCSE Computing and Information Technology.

Trademarks

Android Google, Google Drive, Google Chrome, Gmail, Google Cloud Print and YouTube are trademarks or registered trademarks of Google, Inc. Microsoft Windows, Microsoft Word, Microsoft Publisher, Microsoft Excel and Skype are trademarks or registered trademarks of Microsoft Corporation. Facebook is a registered trade mark of Facebook, Inc. Twitter is a registered trademark of Twitter, Inc. Amazon Kindle is a trademark or registered trademark of Amazon.com, Inc. All other brand and product names used in this book are recognized as trademarks or registered trademarks, of their respective companies.

Acknowledgements

I would like to thank my wife Jill for her support during the preparation of this book and also Michael Babani for making the project possible.

Contents

1

2

5

Entertainment   57

6

Browsing the Web   75

The Android Family

What is an Android?

To science fiction enthusiasts, an Android is a robot designed to look and behave like a human. In the world of tablet computers and smartphones, Android is the name given to the most popular touchscreen *operating system*. Android is owned by Google, famous for its Internet search engine and many other software products.

The Android Operating System

An operating system is a program or collection of programs which controls the basic functions of a computer, such as:

- Connecting to the Internet
- Providing the user interface, such as the touchscreen, icons and menus
- Executing the user's programs or apps
- Displaying information on the screen
- Sending output to a printer
- Saving data on the Internal Storage

The operating system differs from the *applications* software, or *apps* as they are now known, especially in the tablet world. Apps are programs launched for your chosen activity, such as sending an e-mail, playing music or reading an eBook, for example.

The Android operating system is pre-installed on the Internal Storage of a new tablet or smartphone. To keep your Android up-to-date with the latest modifications, you can download and install *updates* from the Internet. Versions of Android are named after confectionery, such as Ice Cream Sandwich (version 4.0), Jelly Bean, (4.1, 4.2, 4.3) and KitKat (4.4).

Android Apps

While the operating system controls the basic functions of the computer, you need software to perform the particular tasks you wish to accomplish. Applications software for laptop and desktop computers has traditionally been bought on CDs or DVDs or downloaded from the software manufacturers' Web sites.

Android tablets, however, have access to nearly a million specially designed apps in the Google Play Store. These can be downloaded from the Internet and installed on your tablet.

If necessary, the installed apps can be used *offline*, i.e. when you are not connected to the Internet, for example where there is no Wi-Fi. Many of the apps are free or cost just a few pounds. Apps are available for a vast range of subjects such as Web browsing, free worldwide telephone calls using Skype, Facebook and Twitter social networking sites, YouTube videos, music, BBC iPlayer television, online newspapers, banking, etc.

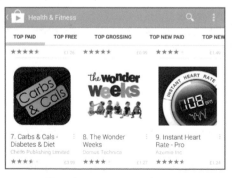

The Google Play Store

Android Tablets

Android was developed from an earlier operating system known as Linux. Some users of laptop and desktop computers prefer Linux to the usual operating system, Microsoft Windows. Linux is also used on very powerful supercomputers. Linux and Android are known as *open-source* operating systems. This means that manufacturers and enthusiasts can access the code for the operating system and, if they wish, modify it to suit their own devices and requirements. This has made Android popular with a wide range of manufacturers of touchscreen devices, initially on smartphones but more recently on tablet computers.

Although the Apple iPad family is currently the most popular single brand of tablet, it's outnumbered by the vast range of Android tablets from many different manufacturers. These include the Google Nexus 7 and 10, the Samsung Galaxy range, the Amazon Kindle and the Tesco Hudl. Most Android tablets are either 7,8 or 10 inches in size, measured diagonally across the screen. Shown below are three very popular Android tablets.

Tesco	Samsung	Google
Hudl	Galaxy Tab 3 10.1	Nexus 7

Android tablets such as the three shown above have a common core of pre-installed icons representing the major tasks and apps. Individual companies may add icons of their own, but most Android tablets are operated in basically the same way.

Some Leading Android Tablets

Nexus 7 and 10

These are marketed by Google in association with the manufacturer Asus. The Android operating system is owned and developed by Google. The Nexus 7 and 10 are light, inexpensive and of very high quality. There is also a range of Nexus mobile phones which use the Android operating system. The Nexus 7 has often been voted the best Android tablet.

Samsung Galaxy Tab and Note

The Galaxy range includes 7, 8 and 10 inch models. The Note tablets have a pen for freehand drawing and writing on the screen. Like the Nexus above, there is also a range of Samsung Galaxy phones, such as the Samsung Galaxy Note 3.

Tesco Hudl

Although this is very inexpensive, it's actually a useful and powerful device. It's not, as might be expected, solely a vehicle for promoting the supermarket giant. While there are a few Tesco specific icons leading to the company's services, the Hudl can be used as a straightforward, competent, 7 inch Android tablet.

Sony Xperia Tablet Z 10.1

This is a very well-regarded and high quality tablet, usually rated near the top of lists of the best Android tablets. Consequently it's more expensive than most other Androids.

The Amazon Kindle Fire

The original Kindle was primarily known as an eBook reader, whereas the Kindle Fire HDX is a more versatile and powerful tablet computer. The Kindle Fire HDX uses the Fire OS operating system, developed by Amazon, but derived from Android.

A free *Kindle app* is available for downloading from the Google Play Store to Android tablets. This enables an Android tablet user to download and read eBooks from the Kindle Store, as well as books from Google's own Play Books store.

The Android User Interface

Android apps are launched by tapping icons on the touch-sensitive screen, using your finger or a *stylus*, a pen-like device with a rubber tip. The Google Nexus 7 uses the standard version of Android, as shown in the Home screen below.

Google Nexus 7

Other makes of tablet, such as the Samsung Galaxy range, the Sony Xperia Tablet Z and the Kindle Fire HDX, use customised versions of Android with some extra features of their own. The Home screen for the Samsung Galaxy is shown below.

Samsung Galaxy Tab 3 10.1

Standard Android Icons

As discussed earlier, some tablets use a modified version of the Android screen, but there is a large common core of apps and their icons which are the same on all Android tablets. Some of the most commonly used apps are listed in the sample below:

 The **Play Store** gives access to thousands of apps in different categories. These are either free or can be bought online for a few pounds then downloaded.

 Google is the world famous *search engine*, used to find information on any subject, after typing or *speaking* relevant *keywords*.

 Google Chrome is a *Web browser* used to display and navigate Web pages. You can retrieve pages you've *bookmarked* or listed in the *browsing history*.

 Google mail or **Gmail** is used to send e-mail messages and pictures. A Gmail account and password gives you access to several other Google services.

 YouTube is a Web site for viewing videos which have been uploaded to the Internet for other people to share.

 Play Music allows you to shop for music to download to your tablet or to play tracks already in your Library.

 Play Movies & TV is used to download and watch videos and TV shows bought from the Play Store.

 Google Drive provides free *cloud* storage space of up to 15GB for photos, etc., and includes **Google Docs** word processing and spreadsheet apps.

 Play Books allows you to read books in your Library or download new ones from a choice of millions in the Play Store, some of them free.

Essential Hardware Terms

The following list describes the main components in Android tablet computers. The first three are present in some form in all types of computer — tablet, laptop and desktop, etc.

Processor

This is a chip which carries out all of the instructions and calculations involved in the execution of the current app or program. The speed of a processor is the rate at which it carries out instructions and is measured in GHz (Gigahertz). Typical tablet processor speeds are between 1GHz and 2.2GHz.

Memory or RAM

This is the temporary store into which the instructions for the current program are loaded. The memory is cleared when the tablet is switched off. A shortage of memory causes a computer to run slowly. Typical memory sizes are between 1GB and 3GB (Gigabytes), similar to many laptop and desktop computers.

Internal Storage

This is not to be confused with the volatile, i.e. temporary, memory or RAM described above. The Internal Storage in a tablet is a location where apps and data files such as photos and music can be permanently saved. The Internal Storage on a tablet usually takes the form of an *SSD* (Solid State Drive). This has no moving parts, in contrast to the hard disc drive on a laptop or desktop computer, which consists of a number of magnetic discs rotating at high speed.

Apps and data files, such as eBooks, which are permanently saved on the Internal Storage, can be accessed offline, i.e. when not connected to the Internet. Typical Internal Storage sizes on a tablet are 8GB, 16GB, 32GB and 64GB. This is very much less than the 500GB to 1000GB or 1TB (Terabyte) common on laptop and desktop computers. The Android tablet compensates for this by saving much of its data in the *clouds* on the Internet, on server computers professionally managed by Google, Inc.

SD Card Slot

Some tablets have a *Micro SD* (Secure Digital) card slot, similar to the SD cards used in cameras. The Micro SD card can be used to supplement the Internal Storage of the tablet. To transfer files between the tablet and the SD card it's necessary to install a *file manager* app, downloadable from the Google Play Store. Typical Micro SD card capacities are 8GB, 16GB, 32GB and 64GB. If you don't have a Micro SD slot you can connect a USB SD card reader via the Micro USB port, discussed below.

Micro USB Port

This is used for connecting a battery charger. It also allows you to connect a tablet computer to a laptop or desktop machine for the transfer of files such as photos, music, videos or text documents. The Micro USB port can also be used to connect devices such as USB SD card readers, mice and keyboards.

Internet Connection

The tablet uses *Wi-Fi*, i.e. radio waves, to connect to the Internet usually via a Wi-Fi router in your home or a Wi-Fi connection provided in a hotel or airport, etc. Some Android tablets have a slot for a 3G or 4G (3rd or 4th Generation) SIM card, providing connection to the Internet via one of the mobile phone networks.

Cameras

A front Webcam, facing the user, allows you to make video calls with Skype, etc. A rear camera, if available, allows the tablet to be used to take photographs and videos in front of the user.

Micro HDMI Port

This allows an Android tablet to display photos and videos, etc., on a High Definition television, projector or computer monitor.

Screen Resolution

The resolution of the screen, usually measured in pixels or dots per inch, affects the sharpness and clarity of the display. The latest Nexus 7 has a resolution of 1920x1200 or 323 pixels per inch. This is one of the highest resolutions on a tablet computer.

Typical Android Tablet Specifications

Shown below are the technical specifications of three popular Android tablets. The Tesco Hudl is a budget tablet, currently selling for around £100 or less, while the Nexus 7 costs around £200, depending on the specification. The Sony Xperia Tablet Z is a high quality machine with some versions costing over £400. The details below are correct at the time of writing, but specifications change as new versions are developed.

	Tesco Hudl	Google Nexus 7	Sony Xperia Tablet Z
Screen size	7ins	7ins	10.1ins
Android O.S.	4.2	4.3, 4.4	4.2 or 4.3
Processor speed	1.5GHz	1.5GHz	1.5GHz
Internal storage	16GB	16 or 32GB	16GB
Memory (RAM)	1GB	2GB	2GB
Screen resolution	1440x900 242dpi	1920x1200 323dpi	1920x1200 224dpi
Front camera Rear camera	2MP 3MP	1.2MP 5MP	2.2MP 8.1MP
Micro USB port	Yes	Yes	Yes
MicroSD slot	32GB	—	32GB
Micro HDMI port	Yes	—	Yes
3G/4G Internet	—	Optional	4G

In the screen resolution above, the first two numbers are the number of *pixels* or dots on the screen in the horizontal and vertical directions and dpi is the number of dots per inch.

Other notable machines include the Kindle Fire HDX, with a processor speed of 2.2GHz and the popular Samsung Galaxy range which comes in 7,8 and 10.1 inch versions.

Additional Information

Certain features were not included in the table on the previous page because they are normally provided as standard on all tablet computers. For example, the 3.5mm audio jack or socket, which allows earphones or headphones to be connected. Similarly the Wi-Fi technology needed to connect to the Internet.

Battery life between charges is important. Figures such as 10-12 hours are quoted, although this depends on what the tablet is being used for — Web browsing, watching videos, etc.

Prices of tablets vary depending on the specification. For example, you may have a choice of 8GB, 16GB, 32GB or 64GB Internal Storage. If you want to save a lot of files on your Internal Storage, e.g. eBooks, music or videos for using offline, then you might prefer to pay extra for a higher storage option.

As shown in the table on the previous page, some tablets have a built-in Micro SD slot for a Micro SD card, providing extra storage of perhaps 32GB or 64GB. The Nexus 7 doesn't have a Micro SD slot. Instead Google provides the *Google Drive* cloud storage system to enable users to store content such as music, video, photos and documents on the Internet. Alternatively, as discussed in detail later in this book, you can connect a USB SD card reader to the Micro USB port, standard on most tablets.

The Android operating system doesn't contain a *file manager* app, needed to copy files to and from a Micro SD card, but a free app is available from the Google Play Store, as discussed later

Some tablets may have an option, at an extra price, to provide 3G or 4G Internet connectivity via a mobile phone network. This allows you to connect to the Internet where there is no Wi-Fi.

The Micro HDMI port listed in the table on the previous page can be used to connect a tablet directly, via a single cable, to a High Definition television, projector or monitor. Tablets without a Micro HDMI port, such as the Nexus 7, can connect to an HD device via the micro USB port, using special cables and adaptors.

Tablets Versus Laptops and Desktops

You could be forgiven for thinking a tiny tablet computer could not possibly be as powerful as the much ˙ bigger laptop and desktop machines. As a regular user of all three computer configurations, I have found that tablets are just as capable at browsing the Internet, playing music and videos, watching live and catchup TV, etc. Two of the critical factors which affect the power and performance of a computer are the processor speed and the amount of memory or RAM. In these two respects, the tablet is just as well equipped as many laptop or desktop machines, with tablet processor speeds ranging from 1GHz to 2.2GHz and RAM sizes typically 1GB, 2GB and even 3GB. Other factors which have enabled the pint-sized tablet computer to seriously damage the sales of laptop and desktop machines are:

- The handy size of the tablet means it can be carried in a small bag or largish pocket and easily used anywhere — on a sofa, in bed, on a train, in a café, etc.

- The tablet doesn't need CDs and DVDs and associated drives. Music, TV, software, etc., can be *downloaded* or *streamed* from the Internet. Thousands of apps and eBooks are available, many of them free or inexpensive.

- The Internal Storage (SSD) of the tablet is much lighter than the hard disc drives in laptops and desktops. A large capacity disc drive is not needed because documents you create are automatically saved in the clouds.

- The keyboard and other peripheral devices such as speakers, microphone, cameras, etc., are integral within the tablet. The tablet does not need heavy duty cables and connecting ports, unlike the desktop machine.

- The tablet has a small, light battery which can typically be used for about 10 hours — much longer than a typical laptop battery, while the desktop machine needs a mains power supply and a bulky built-in power supply unit.

Why Are Android Tablets So Popular?

Android tablets are small, light, fast, inexpensive and easy to use. They are convenient to use anywhere, for very popular or useful activities such as:

- Getting the latest news and weather
- Sending and receiving e-mails and using Skype video calls and social networking
- Listening to music and watching videos, live and catch-up television
- Reading eBooks and online newspapers
- Browsing the Internet to find information on any subject — health, holidays, etc.
- Playing games
- Managing your bank account online
- Buying and selling anything online such as books, holidays, travel tickets

The Future

It's often said that the tablet computer will spell the end for laptop and desktop machines. For the sort of activities listed above, the tablet is the first choice for many people. However, if you need to work at a desk on long documents and complex tasks, the laptop or desktop machine is probably the better option. Depending on your needs, you may need both a tablet and a laptop or desktop machine. Alternatively, as discussed later, you can turn an Android into a desktop replacement computer by connecting a separate keyboard and mouse and a large computer monitor.

Hybrid computers, i.e. a tablet with a detachable keyboard, can be used both as a tablet, e.g. for entertainment, and as a laptop for working. In this context, there are now extra large (12 inch) Samsung Galaxy tablets available, aimed at business users.

Setting Up a New Android Tablet

Introduction

When you open the box containing a new Android tablet, the only other contents are the cable and a special plug for charging the battery and perhaps a couple of flimsy instruction leaflets. As discussed in Chapter 1, the reason the tablet can be so small is the absence of peripheral devices such as disc drives, keyboards and cables, etc. This is possible because the Android uses cloud storage systems on the Internet, such as Google Drive and Dropbox. The clouds are also the main source of software or apps that you may want to download and install.

Charging the Battery

Although the battery may be partially charged on delivery, the instructions usually advise you to charge it further before you get started. One end of the charging cable plugs into the *Micro USB port* on the tablet, as shown on the next page. The other end has a full size USB connector which can be inserted into the special 3-pin 13-amp charger, (provided with the tablet). Alternatively the tablet can be charged by inserting the cable into a USB port on a laptop or desktop computer. This should be carried out with the tablet in sleep mode or switched off. Charging a tablet using a computer is slower than when the Android is connected to a charger plugged into a 13-amp socket.

An Android tablet should last 8-10 hours between charges, depending on the usage — music, browsing, videos, etc.

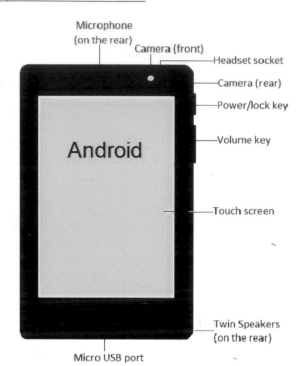

Microphone
(on the rear)
Camera (front)
Headset socket
Camera (rear)
Power/lock key
Volume key
Touch screen
Twin Speakers
(on the rear)
Micro USB port

Connections

The diagram above is based on the Google Nexus 7, but the basic features are the same on all Androids, although their physical locations on the tablet may be different. The Micro USB port is used to charge the battery and to connect external devices such as a flash drive or keyboard. The Micro USB port can also be used to connect an Android tablet to a laptop or desktop computer. The computer can then be used to manage the files on the Android, which doesn't have its own file manager.

Some Androids such as the Samsung Galaxy Tab 10.1 and the Tesco Hudl have a Micro SD card slot for extra storage. The Hudl and the Sony Xperia Tablet Z also have a Micro HDMI port for connecting the tablet to an HD television or monitor. As discussed in Chapter 9, adapters and cables are available to expand tablets which don't have Micro SD or Micro HDMI ports.

Using the Touch Screen

- A single *tap* on an icon opens the app on the screen.

- Tap where you want to enter text and the *on-screen keyboard* pops up ready for you to start typing.

- *Tap and hold* displays a menu relevant to the current screen.

- *Touch and hold* an item such as an app or a widget, before dragging it to a new position with the finger.

- *Swipe* or *slide* a finger across the screen to scroll across Home Screens or unlock the Lock Screen.

- *Pinch* two fingers together to zoom out of a picture or map, etc., or *stretch* the fingers apart to zoom in.

- *Double tap* can be used to zoom in on a map.

Please Note:

- If you find it difficult to use a touch screen with your fingers, you might prefer using a *stylus,* as shown on page 17, for some of the above gestures.

- Instead of entering words using the on-screen keyboard, the Android has a very effective *speech recognition* system, discussed on page 17.

- As discussed in Chapter 9, if you need to do a lot of text entry, you can connect a separate keyboard, mouse and monitor, if necessary.

The On-screen Keyboard

The touch screen method of controlling the computer works very well in most situations. The on-screen keyboard, shown below, pops up whenever you tap in a slot intended for the entry of text.

The standard Android on-screen keyboard

Hide the on-screen keyboard by tapping the icon shown on the right and on the Navigation Bar above.

The Android keyboard above includes a toggle key to switch between numbers and symbols and letters.

The Samsung Galaxy On-screen Keyboard

The Galaxy Android on-screen keyboard

The Galaxy on-screen keyboard displays numbers and letters together, as shown above, unlike the standard Android. The **Sym** key switches on a display of symbols and punctuation marks. Both keyboards display predictive text.

The Stylus

If you find accurate typing difficult using the on-screen keyboard, a cheap *stylus*, (under £2) as shown on the right, may help.

Voice or Speech Recognition

When entering text, for example typing a word you want to search for in Google (discussed later), you will see a small microphone icon, as shown on the right. Tap the microphone icon and after **Speak now** appears, as shown below, begin speaking slowly and clearly.

For example, try saying **Charles Dickens** and you should hear a short spoken extract from Wikipedia, the online encyclopaedia.

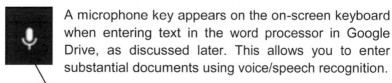 A microphone key appears on the on-screen keyboard when entering text in the word processor in Google Drive, as discussed later. This allows you to enter substantial documents using voice/speech recognition.

The Android microphone key

Starting Up: The Lock Screen

Hold down the Power/lock key, shown on page 14, for a few seconds until the *lock screen* appears as shown below on the Tesco Hudl. *Swipe* the padlock icon by touching it and sliding the finger across the screen.

The Tesco Hudl Lock Screen

On the Samsung Galaxy briefly touch and hold the centre of the screen then swipe across horizontally.

The Samsung Galaxy Lock Screen

Swiping the Lock Screens as described above opens the *Home Screen*, discussed in Chapter 3. Various alternatives to swiping the Lock Screen, such as facial recognition and entering a pin number for extra security, are discussed later in this book.

Connecting to Wi-Fi

You're almost ready to start using the tablet, but with a new computer two more steps are needed — connecting to Wi-Fi and creating a Gmail account.

A Wi-Fi connection is usually made via a *broadband router* in your home or in a hotel or café, etc. Broadband packages with an Internet Service Provider often include a router.

After selecting your language, the Android should automatically detect any available Wi-Fi networks. Alternatively swipe down the screen and tap **SETTINGS**. If necessary tap to set **Wi-Fi** as **ON**. After tapping **Wi-Fi**, you should see a list of available networks.

Available Wi-Fi networks: Standard Android

Samsung Galaxy

The Samsung Galaxy displays a similar window to the standard Android window shown above, but uses its own colour scheme.

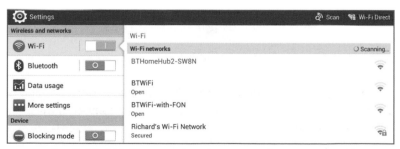

Available Wi-Fi networks: Samsung Galaxy Android

Tap the name of the router or network which you wish to connect to. The keyboard automatically pops up on the screen, enabling you to enter the password for the network, as shown below.

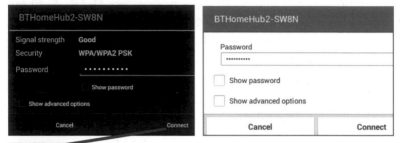

Entering the Wi-Fi Password

Locating the Password

The password can usually be found on the back of a home network router or from the staff of a hotel, etc. Tap **Connect**, shown above, to complete the process of getting online to the Internet. The word **Connected** should now appear below the selected Wi-Fi network, as shown on the next page.

Please Note:

Screenshots with a black background as shown on the left above and elsewhere in this book are in the standard Android format, as used on tablets such as the Nexus 7 and Nexus 10 and the Tesco Hudl.

Screenshots with light backgrounds as shown on the right above are in the TouchWiz format used by the Samsung Galaxy range of tablets.

Checking Your Wi-Fi Connection

You can check your Wi-Fi settings at any time by swiping down from the top right-hand corner of the screen and tapping the **SETTINGS** icon as shown below and in the **Quick Settings** window on page 23. The **SETTINGS** icon has changed on KitKat, currently the latest version of the Android operating system.

KitKat

Jelly Bean

Then tap **Wi-Fi** to display your connection as shown below.

Wi-Fi Connection: Standard Android

Tap the name of the router to see details of the connection.

Samsung Galaxy Settings

On the Samsung Galaxy, tap the **Settings** button at the bottom of the Home screen and shown on the right, to view the Wi-Fi connection as shown below.

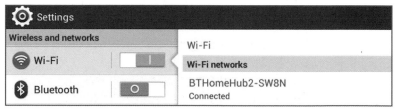

Wi-Fi Connection: Samsung Galaxy Android

Creating a Gmail Account

If you haven't got a Gmail account with an e-mail address and password, you can create one during the initial setting up process for a new Android tablet. It's worth opening a Gmail account because it gives access to several other free Google services, such as Google Drive cloud computing and also Google Docs office software. These topics are discussed later.

You can create a new Google account at any time by swiping down from the top right and selecting **SETTINGS**, as shown on the previous page. Then under **ACCOUNTS**, tap **+Add account**, then tap **Google** and **New**.

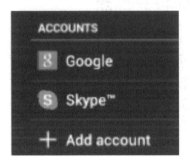 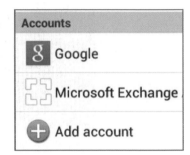

Adding a Google Account

You are then required to enter your first and last name and choose your e-mail address such as:

jimsmith@gmail.com

If your chosen name has already been taken you may need to choose a different name or add some numbers, such as :

jimsmith77@gmail.com

As discussed later, a Google account with Google Drive allows you to access your photos and documents, etc., on any computer anywhere — Android, laptop or desktop PC.

Rotation of the Screen

The screen display can be locked in the vertical or horizontal position or it can rotate automatically when you rotate the tablet. To change the rotation setting, swipe down from the top right of the screen to display the **Quick Settings** window, shown below. Then tap the centre icon, shown on the right, which acts as a toggle switch between the **AUTO ROTATE** and **ROTATION LOCKED** settings.

Quick Settings: Standard Android

Samsung Galaxy Screen Rotation

Swipe down from the top of the screen to display the **Quick Settings** panel shown below. Icons displayed in green are switched on, such as the screen rotation shown on the left and below. Tap an icon to switch the feature on or off.

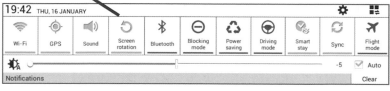

Quick Settings: Samsung Galaxy Android

23

Checking the Battery

The Status Bar at the top right of the screen, shown here on the right, gives a rough indication of the battery life. The other icons show that Bluetooth, W-Fi and Aeroplane mode are switched on, followed on the right by the time.

Alternatively, swipe down from the top right of the screen to display the **Quick Settings** window shown on page 23. The battery icon shown on the right is on the centre right of the **Quick Settings** window.

Samsung Galaxy

Tap the **Settings** icon at the bottom of the Home screen. Then scroll the left-hand panel upwards and tap **Battery**, as shown below.

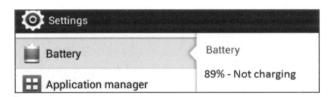

Checking the state of the battery: Samsung Galaxy Android

Shutting Down

Hold down the Power/Lock key shown on page 14, until the following window appears. Then tap **Power off** as shown below, followed by tapping **OK** to finish the shut down.

 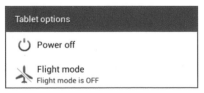

Shutting down

Finding Your Way Around

The Home Screens

Start the Android tablet by holding down the Power button. Then swipe the Lock Screen, as discussed in Chapter 2. The next screen you see is the central *Home Screen*, as shown below.

Standard Android   Samsung Galaxy

The Central Home Screen

There are actually several Home Screens on an Android tablet. The central Home Screen has a number of preinstalled apps. The other Home Screens are initially blank panels which you can customise by adding apps from the Play Store. You can move between the various Home Screens by swiping left or right.

The Favorites Tray

Along the bottom of all the Home Screens is the *Favorites Tray*
shown below, giving quick access to frequently used apps.

Favorites Tray: Standard Android

The Samsung Galaxy uses a Shortcuts Bar, shown below, which
is used in a very similar way to the Favorites Tray.

Shortcuts Bar: Samsung Galaxy

As you can see, the Favorites Tray and the Shortcuts Bar have
some icons in common and these can be changed, if necessary,
to give quick access to your own frequently used apps.

The All Apps Icons

The All Apps icon shown on the right appears on the
Favorites Tray. Tapping this icon opens the Apps
screen shown on the next page on the left. A similar
Apps icon shown here on the lower right appears on
the Galaxy Shortcuts Bar above.

These All Apps icons are permanent fixtures on the
Favorites Tray and the Shortcuts Bar, respectively.

The Apps Screens

In addition to the Home Screens, there are several Apps screens. These contain a number of apps preinstalled on a new tablet. In addition you can install further apps from the Google Play Store. Sample Apps screens for the standard Android and the Samsung Galaxy are shown below. The Apps screens are launched by the All Apps icons which appear on the Favorites Tray and the Shortcuts Bar, as shown on the previous page.

Standard Android   Samsung Galaxy

The Apps Screens

There are normally two or three Apps screens and icons are added as you obtain new apps from the Play Store. Icons can be copied from the Apps screens to blank spaces on your Home Screens. You can then create personal Home Screens for different activities such as entertainment or work, etc.

Widgets

At the top of the Apps screen, there is a tab labelled **WIDGETS**.

Widgets appear on the screen like Apps but usually display information which is regularly updated. Typical uses of widgets are:

- Local weather forecasts
- Your e-mail inbox
- An analogue or digital clock
- Newspaper headlines and articles
- A calendar
- Local traffic reports
- A battery charge indicator

Many widgets are already preinstalled on a new Android tablet and more can be downloaded and installed from the Play Store. You can create a special screen just for the widgets you find especially useful. As discussed shortly, apps and widgets can be copied, moved about and deleted.

Navigating the Screens

The Navigation Bar shown below is used to switch between the different screens, in addition to the methods of swiping left or right or tapping the All Apps icons shown on page 26. The Navigation Bar appears along the bottom of all the Home Screens.

Navigation buttons: Standard Android

- The left-hand button above opens the previous screen.
- The button in the middle opens the central Home Screen.
- The right-hand button displays thumbnails of previously visited screens. Tap a thumbnail to open the full screen.

Samsung Galaxy

The navigation buttons on the Samsung Galaxy Tab 3 10.1 are slightly different and are located in the bezel or frame of the Galaxy as shown below.

Navigation buttons: Samsung Galaxy

- The left-hand button displays a menu of options relevant to the current screen.
- The raised middle button opens the central Home Screen.
- The right-hand button displays the previous screen.

Shortcut Icons for Popular Android Apps

 All Apps: displays all the apps installed on a tablet.

 Google Chrome: a Web browser for navigating the Internet.

 Google Play Store: the source for downloading apps.

 Google: *search engine* used to find information on any subject.

 Google Earth: photos and satellite images of places around the world, including Google Street View.

 Google Mail or **Gmail**: an electronic mail service.

 Email: electronic mail services of your choice.

 Play Music: install and play music, create playlists.

 Play Movies & TV: rent or buy then download.

 Google Maps: Searchable maps of the world with facilities to zoom in and zoom out.

Camera: a second camera on the back of an Android tablet suitable for general photography.

 Google Drive: cloud storage area which also includes free word processing and spreadsheet software.

 Dropbox: cloud storage area allowing photos and files, etc., to be accessed from any computer.

 Play Books: Download and read eBooks from the Google Play Store and create your own library.

 Kindle: Download and read eBooks from the Amazon Kindle Store.

 Skype: Internet telephone service allowing free video calls between computers around the world.

 Facebook: the popular social networking Web site.

 Twitter: social networking using "tweets" or short messages.

 Hangouts: send messages to your friends or start a video call.

 People: manage all your e-mail contacts, etc., and add information to their records.

 Google+: a social network allowing you to share updates and photos, etc.

Currents: displays news headlines and reports.

 Calculator: an easy to use basic calculator.

 Calendar: record future events, birthdays, etc., and receive notifications when imminent.

 Downloads: view documents, etc., that you've previously downloaded from the Internet.

 Gallery: view and manage your photographs.

 Clock: view the time in cities around the world and also use as an alarm clock and stopwatch.

 BBC iPlayer: watch live and catchup television.

 YouTube: watch free videos, e.g. amusing incidents, uploaded to the Internet for other people to share.

 Cloud Print: use the Web to print from anywhere to any printer.

The Google Play Store

Many of the apps listed on the previous three pages are standard on all Android tablets, while there are some that I have downloaded from the Play Store. Some tablet manufacturers also include default apps of their own and Samsung has its own apps store for users of Galaxy tablets.

The Google Play Store is the main source of Android apps, with hundreds of thousands of apps for a wide variety of activities.

To launch the **Play Store**, tap its icon (shown on the right) on the Home Screen. The **Google Play** window opens, showing the six subject areas **APPS**, **GAMES**, **MOVIES**, **MUSIC**, **BOOKS** and **NEWSSTAND**.

If, for example, you tap **APPS** and swipe or scroll from left to right, you can see the main **CATEGORIES** of apps down the left-hand side, such as **Games** and **Business**, shown below.

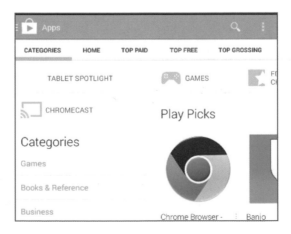

Browsing the Play Store

For example, tap **CATEGORIES** shown on the previous page and then tap **Finance**, towards the middle of the **CATEGORIES** column. Various groups of apps are available such as **TOP PAID**, **TOP FREE**, **TOP GROSSING**, etc., on the bar across the top of the screen, as shown below.

Entertainment

Finance

Health & Fitness

The screen shot below shows some of the apps displayed after selecting **TOP FREE** in the **Finance** category.

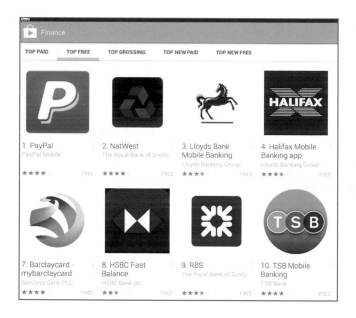

Some apps display the word **FREE**, otherwise a price is displayed.

Tap an icon, as shown above, to display a detailed description of the app and its functions as shown at the top of the next page.

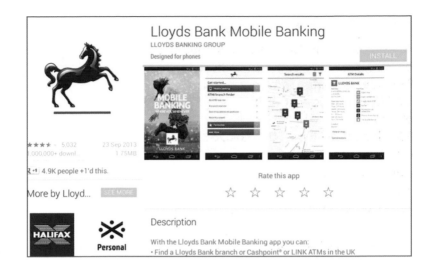

Downloading and Installing an App

If the app is free, the **INSTALL** button is displayed, as shown on the right and above. If there is a charge for an app, tap the price and you can then buy the app after providing your bank details. After you buy an app, the **INSTALL** button is displayed.

Tap the **INSTALL** button to download a copy of the app to your tablet. A shortcut icon for the app, Lloyds Bank in this example, is placed on your Apps screen and on your Home Screen. Tap the icon to start using the app.

Widgets are downloaded from the Play Store and installed in a similar way to apps, as described above.

Searching the Play Store for Apps

Tap the icon shown on the right to open the Play Store.
Then tap **APPS**, as shown on the **Google Play** window
on page 33. Next tap the magnifying glass search icon,
as shown on the right.

Typing Keywords

The search bar appears as shown below, with a flashing cursor
ready for you to type the name of the app or widget you wish to
search for. The on-screen keyboard pops up automatically. Enter
the keywords for the search, such as **flight simulator**, for
example, and tap the search key (displaying a magnifying glass
search icon) on the on-screen keyboard.

Using the Microphone: Speech Recognition

Tap the microphone icon shown on the right. The small
window shown below appears, requiring you to speak
the keywords, such as **flight simulator**.

You might like to practise searching for a few apps using the
microphone. Apps I found in this way included **chess game**,
route planner and **sound recorder**, for example.

Having found an app that you require, follow the instructions on
the previous page to download the app and install on your tablet.

Customising the Favorites Tray

The Favorites Tray on the standard Android is shown below. The All Apps icon shown on the right and below is a fixture on the Favorites Tray — it cannot be moved or deleted. The other six icons can be moved and replaced with any other apps you prefer.

As shown on page 26, instead of the Favorites Tray, the Samsung Galaxy uses a Shortcuts Bar, which is very similar.

Removing an App from the Favorites Tray

Touch and hold the app you want to remove from the Favorites Tray until **X Remove** appears at the top of the screen. Drag the icon over **X Remove** and drop it, deleting the app. Removing an app from the Favorites Tray doesn't uninstall the app from the All Apps screen. Alternatively, move an app from the Favorites Tray and slide it onto another part of the Home Screen.

Moving an App to the Favorites Tray

Clear a space on the Favorites Tray by moving or removing an icon, as described above. To move an app on the Home Screen to the Favorites Tray, tap and hold the icon, then drag the icon to the space on the Favorites Tray. In the example below, the green **Hangouts** icon shown above has been removed and replaced by the shopping bag icon for the Play Store. The **Maps** app (third from the left above) has been replaced by a *folder* which includes the **Facebook** app. Folders are discussed on page 40.

Customising Your Home Screen

When you start using a new Android tablet, you can tailor the Home Screen to suit your own requirements, as follows:

- Change the background colour or wallpaper.
- Copy apps from the Apps screen and place them on a personal page on the Home Screen.
- Delete any apps and widgets you no longer need.

The Home Screen actually consists of several separate panels or pages, some of which are initially blank. You can group apps into *folders*, which can be added to the Home Screen and to the Favourites Tray. Folders are discussed on page 40.

Changing the Wallpaper on Your Home Screen

Hold your finger on an empty part of the Home Screen until the window shown below appears. Tap any of the icons to view the available choices. **Gallery** displays your own photos, **Live Wallpaper** presents moving objects and **Wallpaper** includes various patterns such as the background shown on page 40. For example, tap **Wallpaper** shown below and then tap your chosen pattern. Then tap **Set wallpaper** to apply the new background.

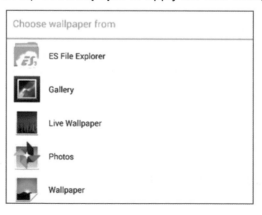

Adding Apps to Your Home Screen

To make up a personal Home Screen displaying only the apps you find most useful, open the Home Screen where you want the apps to appear. Clear the screen of any apps and widgets you don't want. This is done by touching and holding the app or widget, then dragging onto **X Remove**, as described previously.

Tap the All Apps icon as shown on the right then touch and hold the app you want to move to the Home Screen. The Home Screen opens. Keeping your finger on the app, slide it into the required position on the Home Screen. Part of a personal Home Screen is shown below.

A Personal Home Screen

Deleting Apps from the Home Screen

Tap and hold an unwanted app until **X Remove** appears at the top of the screen. Then drag the app over **X Remove** to delete it. Apps deleted from the Home Screen are only *copies* — the apps still exist on the Apps screen.

Unlike apps removed from the Home Screen, apps *uninstalled* from the Apps screen are completely removed from the tablet. If the uninstalled apps are needed in the future, they will need to be reinstalled from the *Play Store*.

Organising Apps in Folders

Folders containing several apps, as shown on the right, can be created on the Home Screen and on the Favorites bar. For example, you could put the apps for **Facebook**, **Twitter** and **Skype**, shown below on the Home Screen, in a folder called **Social**.

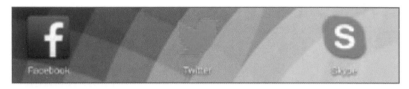

Touch and drag the icons, one on top of the other, to form a single circular folder icon shown on the left below. Tap the folder icon to reveal the contents and to give a name to the folder. As shown below, tap **Unnamed Folder** and enter a name of your choice, **Social** in this example. Tap a folder icon to view and launch the individual apps within, as shown in the middle below.

Samsung Galaxy

Tap and hold an empty part of the Home Screen and select **Folder** from the menu which pops up. Then enter a name, such as **Social** in this example, in the **Create Folder** window shown below and then tap **OK**. To place an app in the new folder, touch and hold the app then drag and drop it over the folder.

More Android Features

Introduction

Previous chapters have looked at the setting up of an Android tablet and the apps and widgets which are used to drive these small but extremely powerful and versatile devices. This chapter describes some more of the very useful features built into the Android operating system.

Google Now and Google Cards

These features enable Google to search for information using both voice and text queries. Google Cards automatically displays useful, real-time information for your current location.

Settings

Used to switch important settings on and off, make adjustments and tailor the Android to your own requirements.

Notifications

This screen keeps you up-to-date with new e-mail messages, calendar events, new downloads, Bluetooth, Wi-Fi, battery strength and aeroplane mode, as discussed shortly.

My Library

This is a widget that displays all the books, movies, music, etc., that are already on your Android tablet.

Calendar

Keeps track of all your appointments and sends reminders of imminent events, synchronised to your various devices.

Google Now

This is an extension to the popular Google search engine. Google Now employs GPS (Global Positioning System) satellite technology to pinpoint your current location. This is used to gather local information such as the weather and traffic conditions.

Google Now doesn't require any setting up. You just need to make sure **Google Now** is switched on in the **Settings** window, together with **Location access**, **GPS satellites** and **Wi-Fi**, as discussed on page 47 and 48.

To open Google Now, swipe up from the bottom of the screen, or tap the Google icon on the Home Screen, shown on the right. If Google Now is switched on, the colourful screen shown below opens with a search bar across the top.

In the centre of the screen above is a *Google Card*. This is a small panel which pops up, showing local information and subjects of personal interest such as news of your favourite sports teams. Google Cards are discussed shortly.

Searching in Google Now

Typing Keywords

Enter the keywords for a search, such as **weather in los gigantes**, by typing into the search bar at the top of the screen, using the on-screen keyboard.

Spoken Queries

You can also tap the microphone icon, as shown above and on the right. Then speak your query into the tablet. Using spoken queries is discussed in more detail on page 36. The search produces a spoken answer, as well as a Google Card, as shown above. You will also see some traditional Google results, as shown below, which you can tap to open Web pages relevant to your search.

> **Weather in Los Gigantes,** Canary Islands
> www.holiday-weather.com › Europe › Canary Islands
> Los Gigantes is a stunning location in Tenerife in the Canary Islands. It is blessed with spectacular views and breathtaking scenery. The **weather in** Los Gigantes ...

Perhaps you could experiment with a few spoken queries. For example, I spoke the question, "what is an android?". I received the spoken answer, "In science fiction a robot with a human appearance." This also appeared on a Google Card together with a list of traditional Google search results, as shown below.

Sporting Fixtures

If you enter or speak the name of a favourite sports team, such as Manchester City, Google Now produces a list of their latest results, news and fixtures, in both spoken and text form.

Local Information

Similarly you could ask for a forecast of tomorrow's weather, traffic conditions on a particular route or a list of restaurants in your area or in your current location (if using Wi-Fi on the move).

More on Google Cards

Google Cards pop up on the Google Now screen without you taking any action. For example, suppose you enquire about flights at your local airport, or about traffic on local roads. Google Now responds with Google Cards based on your recent activity.

As shown above, Google Cards report on the volume of traffic on the relevant roads and may give a time and a link to a suggested route to a destination, such as an airport. If you tap an information icon, as shown on the right and above, a panel appears at the bottom of the card, as shown below. This explains why the Google Card has been displayed.

You've recently searched for Birmingham Airport, Birmingham, Birmingham, B26 3QJ

Sample Google Cards

At the bottom of the Google Now screen, you often see the message, **Show sample cards**. Tap this message to see a list of topics for which Google Cards are available, together with examples. As you can see from the list of sample cards below, Google Cards are available on a wide range of subjects, such as **Weather**, **Traffic**, **Public transport**, etc.

Flight Information

I recently made a Google enquiry about a flight from Frankfurt to Birmingham. Shortly afterwards on the same day a Google Card popped up with the latest flight information, as shown below.

Settings for Google Now

Google Now requires the following settings:

- Google Now **ON**
- Location access **ON**
- GPS satellites **ON**
- Wi-Fi & mobile location **ON**

If **Google Now** is not **ON**, when you swipe up from the bottom, or tap the **Google** icon on the Home Screen, you only see the basic Google screen, not the more colourful **Google Now** screen, as shown on page 42. To turn **Google Now ON**, tap the menu icon shown on the right and below, at the bottom of the Google screen. (You may need to swipe up to see it).

Show more cards...

From the menu which appears, tap **Settings** and then make sure **Google Now** is **ON**. If necessary tap the **ON/OFF** button and then tap **Yes, I'm in**.

On the Samsung Galaxy Tab press the menu button on the bezel or frame, shown on the right and on page 29, then tap **Settings** and make sure **Google Now** is **ON**.

Switching the Location Service, GPS and Wi-Fi ON

Swipe down from the top right of the screen, to display the **Quick Settings** panel. Then select **SETTINGS** and under **PERSONAL** tap **Location access**. The three settings to enable Google Now to pinpoint your current location are shown below and should be **ON** or ticked. Tap anywhere in a row to change a setting.

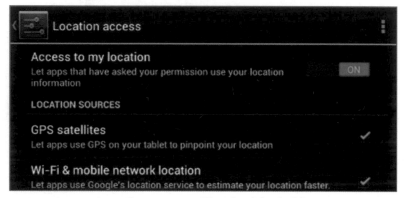

Location access: Standard Android

Samsung Galaxy

The corresponding window on the Samsung Galaxy Tab is opened by tapping the **Settings** icon, shown on the right, on the bottom of the Home screen. Then scroll the left-hand panel upwards, tap **Location services** and make sure all the settings shown below are on.

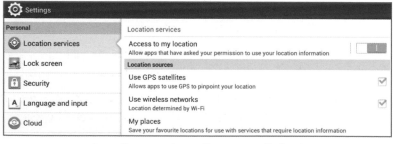

Location services: Samsung Galaxy

Quick Settings

Swipe down from the top right of the screen, to display the Quick Settings window shown below.

- The image at the top left opens your Google Profile.

- **SETTINGS** opens the list shown on the next page. (As shown on page 21, Jelly Bean uses a different icon).

- Tap **WI-FI OFF** to connect to a network. (If you're already on a network, the name is shown instead of **WI-FI OFF**).

- **AUTO ROTATE** keeps the screen display upright when you turn the tablet through 90 degrees. Tap and select **ROTATION LOCKED** to fix the display to the tablet sides.

- **65%** shown above is the level of charge left in the battery.

- **AEROPLANE MODE** (or **FLIGHT MODE**) switches off the Internet so that the tablet can be safely used on a flight.

- **BLUETOOTH**, when **ON**, allows two *paired* devices to connect wirelessly over short distances, to exchange data.

- **LOCATION** opens the various settings discussed on the previous page to pinpoint your exact location.

The Main Android Settings Screen

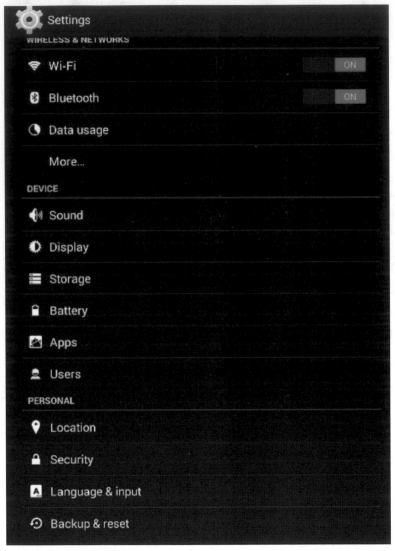

It's necessary to swipe upwards to display the bottom part of the Settings menu, as shown on the next page.

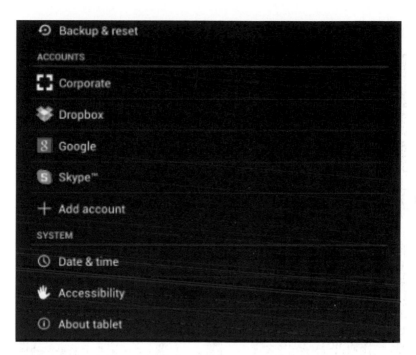

The Settings menu allows you to check your Wi-Fi and any Bluetooth connections. **Apps** on the previous page lists all your applications and gives you the chance to disable them. **Users** allows the addition of profile information.

Location is where you can set up GPS, so that you can access local information. **Security** has many options including the setting of a password required to start using the tablet. Other settings include the creation of accounts on Skype, Dropbox and Google, etc. **Accessibility** provides help for those with special needs such as poor eyesight, etc.

Samsung Galaxy Settings

The settings are opened using the icon shown on page 48 and are very similar to the standard Android settings above and on the previous page, although different in colour and appearance.

Notifications and System Icons

Across the top of the Home and All Apps screens you should see two groups of very small icons.

The group on the left above represent events such as receiving an e-mail, capturing a screenshot or events from your calendar (discussed shortly). The group of small icons on the right above are *system icons*. The icons in this group change according to your settings. For example, icons may be present which show Bluetooth ON, sound OFF, Aeroplane Mode ON, Wi-Fi ON, the battery state of charge and the current time.

To display your notifications, as shown in the examples below, swipe down from the top left of the screen. If a notification refers to an e-mail, tap to read the message. Once you've looked at a notification, it's removed from the list.

Tapping the icon, shown on the right and at the top right below, dismisses all notifications.

Notifications: Standard Android

Notifications: Samsung Galaxy

My Library

This is a widget that displays all the music, magazines, books, and movies that are installed on an Android tablet. If necessary, clear a space on the Home Screen by deleting unwanted apps and widgets as described on page 39.

To install the **My Library** widget, tap the **All Apps** icon shown on the right and then tap **WIDGETS** at the top. Swipe to the left until you see the **Play – My Library** widget as shown below left. Touch and hold this widget, then slide into a space on the Home Screen. The **Play-My Library** window opens as shown below on the right.

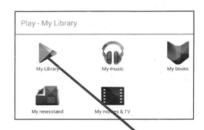

Tap the **MY LIBRARY** icon, shown on the right and in the window above right, to save thumbnails for all of your installed media — **My music**, **My books** and **My newsstand**, etc., on the Home Screen as shown on the right. Tap a thumbnail in **My Library** to read a book, listen to music or watch a movie, for example.

If you tap individual icons such as **My music** or **My books**, shown above on the right, separate widgets for each medium are placed on the Home Screen, rather than all of your media stored in **My Library**.

The notes on this page also apply to the Samsung Galaxy

The Google Calendar

The Android Calendar has many useful features such as:

- Keeping a record of all your future events.
- Sending you notifications of imminent events.
- Synchronizing changes between various devices, such as your Android, smartphone, laptop or desktop PC or Mac.

The Calendar can be opened by tapping its icon on the Apps screen, as shown on the right.

The Calendar opens as shown in the example on the right, displaying the events for the current week. An arrow at the top, next to **Week**, opens a menu enabling you to display **Day**, **Week**, **Month** or an **Agenda** listing all of your events. When a **Day** or a **Week** are displayed, the current month is also displayed at the bottom left, as shown on the right. You can scroll through displays of the days or weeks by swiping horizontally. To scroll through a display of the months, swipe vertically.

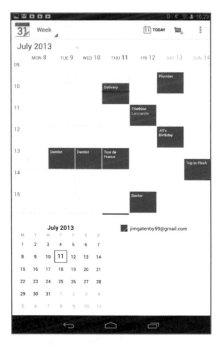

Creating a New Event

Tap the icon at the top of the calendar or tap twice in the correct hourly slot on the appropriate day. The **New Event** screen appears as shown below. Here you can enter the name of the event and the location, time and the names of any guests.

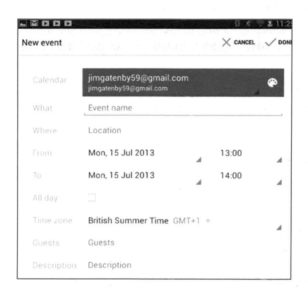

At the bottom of the **New event screen** shown above, (visible when the keyboard is not displayed), you can set a **Reminder** in the form of a notification or an e-mail. With a notification there is a beep and then an event, such as **Barbecue** in this example, appears in the **Notifications** panel, as discussed on page 52. Tap the event name, as shown below, for further details.

The Calendar Widget

A Calendar widget appears in the WIDGETS section of the All Apps screen and this can be placed on a suitable clear space on the Home Screen. This is done by touching and holding the widget and then sliding into position on the Home Screen, as described on page 53. The widget lists all your forthcoming events, automatically updated with information from the Calendar app. Tap the Calendar widget to open the Calendar app for editing.

The Calendar Widget

Syncing Your Android Calendar with a PC, etc.

The Google Calendar can be viewed on all the common platforms — Android, iPad, laptop or desktop, PC or Mac, etc. Just open **www.google.co.uk**. You must be signed in with your Gmail address. Then select the **Apps** icon on the top right of the screen, shown here on the right. From the drop-down window which appears, select the **Calendar** icon, shown below, to open the Calendar.

Google icons displayed on a laptop PC

New events added to the Calendar on any of your computers are automatically synced across to all your other machines.

Entertainment

Introduction

Amongst many other things, the Android tablet is a versatile entertainment platform. The following activities are discussed in this chapter:

- eBooks — electronic books which may be downloaded from the Internet for reading offline at any time.

- Music, magazines, movies and games downloaded for free or bought or rented.

- YouTube — a Google-owned Web site enabling you to play free music and videos uploaded by other people.

- Live and catchup TV and radio.

The small size and light weight of an Android tablet means you can use it literally anywhere — on a sofa, in bed or in a public place such as a restaurant. You can stow it in a bag and take it on holiday; most hotels now have free Wi-Fi so while you're away you can still go online for all your favourite Internet activities. The Android tablet may also be used for your personal in-flight entertainment, if the airline allows it. *Aeroplane mode* or *flight mode* should be switched on to prevent possible interference with the aircraft's instruments. This was mentioned on page 49 and only allows you to use the tablet *offline*, i.e. not connected to the Internet. Such offline activities would include reading an e-Book or watching movies which have been saved on the internal storage of the tablet, before boarding the aircraft.

eBooks

The Amazon Kindle, introduced in 2007, was a pioneer in the reading of electronic books or *eBooks*, especially on tablet computers. The Kindle uses its own heavily modified version of the Android operating system.

Millions of eBooks are available to be downloaded from the Amazon Kindle Store and saved on a tablet such as the Kindle Fire, the Apple iPad or Androids such as the Nexus 7 or Samsung Galaxy tab. A tablet can keep more books on its internal storage than most people are ever likely to read.

- Android has its own app, *Play Books*, for reading eBooks and you can use it to download books from the Google Play Store, which contains millions of titles.

- You can also install the free Kindle App for Android tablets and obtain books from the Amazon Kindle Store.

You can always delete any eBooks you no longer want, to save space on the internal storage of the tablet.

Google Play Books

When you first start to use an Android tablet, there is already an icon for the Play Books app on the Apps screen. If you read a lot of eBooks you may wish to copy the icon to the Favorites Tray as shown below, if it is not already there.

Tap the Play Books app shown at the bottom of the previous page. On a brand new Android, you'll probably find a few books are already installed, as shown below in **My Library**.

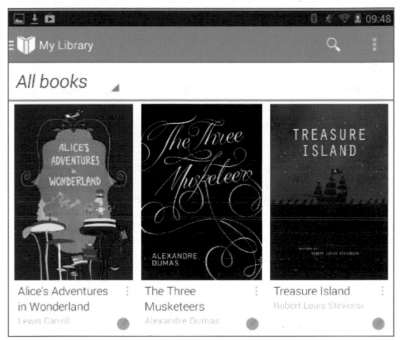

Tap **Read now** or **My Library** (whichever is shown on the top left of the screen) to display the menu shown on the right, which includes the **Shop** option. Tap **Shop** to open the Play Store as shown on the next page.

The Play Store can also be opened by tapping its shopping bag icon shown on the right below and on the right of the Favorites Tray on the previous page.

In the Play Store, as shown below, you can browse through the various categories listed down the left-hand side, check new arrivals and best selling books or look at the top free books.

Alternatively you can search for a particular book after tapping the search icon shown on the right and above. Type in the title of the book, replacing **Search Google Play** shown below. Or tap the microphone icon shown in the middle below and speak the title of the book.

For example, a search for **cats** produced numerous results, as shown in the small sample below. Tap a book cover for more details or to buy the book.

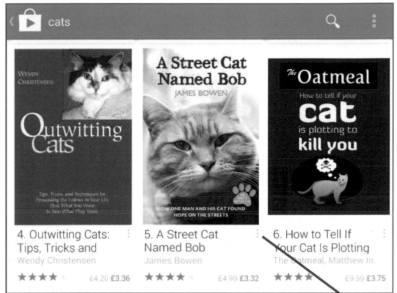

Alternatively tap the small three dot menu shown on the right and above, to the right of the book title, to add the book to a wish list or to buy it.

To make sure you can read a book offline, display the book in **My Library**, as discussed at the bottom of page 59 and tap the three dot menu icon shown below the book cover. If necessary, tap **Keep on device** to make the book available to be read offline. The pin icon will then be white and vertical, as shown below.

Reading an eBook

Tap the Books app on the Favorites Tray, or on the Apps screen, to open My Library, as discussed on page 59. Then tap the cover of the book you want to read. The book opens on the screen at the first page. Scroll backwards and forwards through the pages by swiping to the left or right.

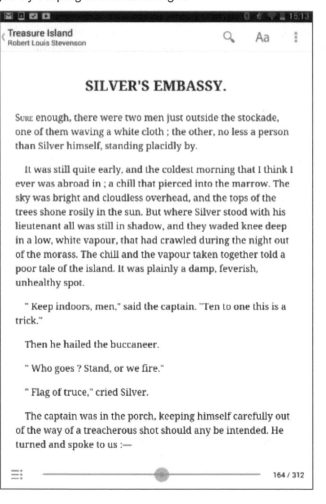

Tap anywhere on the screen to view information about the current page you are reading, as shown below.

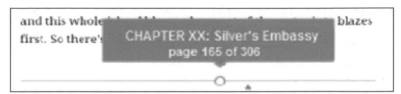

Drag the blue circle on the scroll bar to advance rapidly forward or backward through the book. A blue triangle marks the page you were previously reading.

The menu bar across the top of the eBook page, as shown above and on the previous page, includes the following icons:

Q   Search for certain words and highlight them where they occur in the text.

Aa   Change the brightness, type size and typeface.

⋮   Open the menu shown on the right, which includes options to **bookmark** a page in the text.

≡⋮   This icon, also shown at the bottom left of the previous page, lists chapter headings,   page   numbers   and bookmarks. You can view and return to the bookmarked pages after tapping this icon. You can also **Share** the book with someone else, using social networking or e-mail.

Read aloud on the menu at the bottom of the previous page turns the Android tablet into a *talking book*. The **Settings** option on the menu displays the window shown below. This includes options to turn **read aloud** on when an **accessibility** setting is on and to **Use the volume keys to turn pages**.

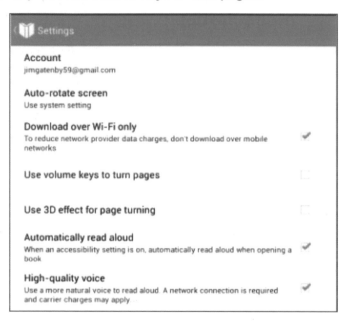

Original pages shown on the menu at the bottom of the previous page displays a book in the style of the original paper edition of the book, as shown in the extract below.

> ## CHAPTER XXV.
>
> ### I STRIKE THE JOLLY ROGER.
>
> I HAD scarce gained a position on the bowsprit, when the flying jib flapped and filled upon the other tack, with a report like a gun. The schooner trembled to her keel under the reverse; but next moment, the other sails

Access to eBooks and Other Media Offline

The Android tablet automatically stores all the eBooks (and other media such as music, etc.,) in your library in the clouds on the Internet. This makes them very rapidly available when you are connected to Wi-Fi. However, if you want to read the books *offline* (e.g. in Aeroplane Mode as discussed earlier, or where there is no Wi-Fi), the books, etc., need to be saved on the internal storage of the tablet. Tap the **Play Books** icon on the Home Screen or on the Favorites Tray shown on page 58. With the **My Library** screen selected, tap the small three dot menu icon to the right of the name of each book, as shown on the right and on the left-hand image below. This displays a small menu, as shown on the right below.

Keep on device

Delete from library

About this book

Tap **Keep on device**, shown above, to retain access to your eBooks, etc., when you are not connected to Wi-Fi.

Deleting eBooks and Other Media

Tap **Delete from library** shown above and below, to remove the eBook or music, etc., from your library in the clouds. The **Don't keep** option appears on the menu shown on the right, if an eBook or music, etc., has been previously saved on the internal storage of the tablet, for reading offline. Tapping **Don't keep** removes the eBook or music, etc., from the internal storage of the Android.

Don't keep

Delete from library

About this book

The Kindle App for Android Tablets

To read eBooks in the popular Kindle format, it's just a case of installing the Kindle app from the Google Play Store. Tap the Play Store shopping bag icon, shown on

the right above and on the Favorites Tray or on the Apps Screen. Then tap **APPS** and tap the magnifying glass search icon. Type **Kindle** into the search bar or tap the microphone icon and say **Kindle** to display a list of

Kindle apps, as shown in the small sample above.

Tap the Amazon Kindle app shown on the left above and tap **INSTALL** to put an icon, shown on the right, on your Apps and Home Screens. Sign in with your

Amazon e-mail address and password or create a new account if necessary.

To start reading one of the Kindle books tap the book's front cover.

Tap **Store** at the top right of the screen to open the Amazon Book Store of over 2 million books. If you already have an account with Amazon, you can buy books very easily using **Buy Now with 1-Click**.

The Android Newsstand

Select **NEWSSTAND** in the Play Store as shown on page 33. Here you can choose from a wide range of magazines and newspapers in various categories.

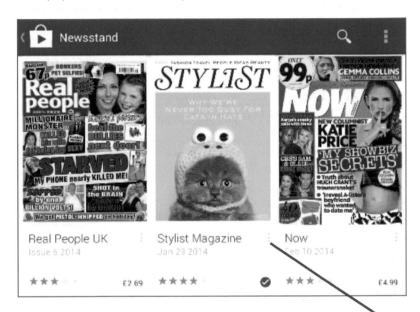

Tap the three dot menu button to the right of the name of a magazine or newspaper, etc., shown here on the right and above. This opens the small menu shown below on the right, allowing you to buy a single issue or take out a monthly or yearly subscription.

Subscribe
Buy issue £2.49
Add to wishlist

After you've chosen to buy or subscribe, tap **Install** to place a copy of the news media in your **Play Newsstand**. You will then be able to access the magazine or newspaper, etc., after tapping the **Play Newsstand** icon on your Apps Screen, as shown on the right.

Reading a Magazine

Tap the **Play Newsstand** icon, as shown on the right, on your Apps Screen. Tap in the top left-hand corner of the Newsstand window to display the menu shown below on the right.

Play Newsstand

Read Now produces lists of the latest news headlines. Tap a headline to read the full article. **My News** displays a selection of well-known newspapers. Tap **My Magazines** to display lots of journals as shown in the small sample below. Tap the three dot menu shown on the previous page and then select **Keep on device**

to enable the magazine to be viewed offline, as discussed on page 65 and elsewhere.

To start reading a magazine, tap the front cover as show above. Tap anywhere on a page to display the icon shown on the right and below. Tapping this displays thumbnails of the various pages. Drag the circular blue slider, shown below, to move through the pages of the magazine.

The Music App

Open the Play Store as discussed on page 33 and tap **MUSIC**. Then browse the various **GENRES** of music, such as **Classical**, **Folk** or **Pop** and **TOP ALBUMS** or **TOP SONGS**, etc.

Alternatively tap the magnifying glass search icon, shown below, then enter the name of a piece of music or an artist.

 Tap the cover picture to buy a single or album. Or tap the three dot menu icon which, in this example, has options to **Add to wishlist** or **Buy £0.99**.

The music you buy is added to your library. Then it can be played after tapping the Play Music icon shown on the left and located on the Apps Screen.

The control bar along the bottom of the music screen has the usual Play, Forward, Back and Pause buttons, as shown below.

The volume key is located on the side of a tablet as shown on page 14, although the precise position of the key is different on some Android tablets. Tap the three dot menu icon on the front cover and tap **Keep on device** to save the music on the internal storage of your tablet, for viewing offline.

Movies on the Android

The Play Store contains a range of movies and TV shows in various categories. Some can be bought or rented while others can only be rented. You may have to begin watching a movie within 30 days of renting it and the rental may expire 48 hours after you start watching it.

Tap **RENT** or **BUY** then select **PLAY** or **DOWNLOAD**.

To watch a movie you've bought or rented, tap the **Play Movies & TV** icon shown on the right, which appears on the Apps screen, then tap **PLAY**.

Downloading for Offline Viewing – the Pin Icon

To make a movie watchable offline, tap the angled pin icon shown on the right, on the movie artwork. This starts downloading the movie. The pin icon starts to fill with colour and, when completely full, the download is complete. The pin icon is now white and vertical, as shown on the right. A notification should also be displayed when you swipe down from the top left-hand corner of the screen, as discussed on page 52.

The YouTube App

YouTube is a Web site, owned by Google, which provides a platform for people to share videos which they've recorded themselves. These can rapidly become very popular and "go viral", watched by millions of people around the world.

To launch YouTube, tap the icon shown on the right, on the Apps screen. The YouTube screen shows a long list of video clips which can be scrolled up and down by swiping. Swipe from left to right to display the categories menu shown below.

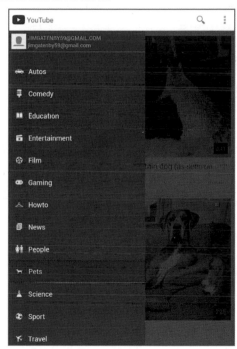

Tap a menu option such as **Pets** and, if necessary, scroll vertically to display the cover picture of a video you want to watch. Tap the picture to start the video. To pause a video, tap the screen and then tap the pause button.

Live and Catchup Television and Radio

The Google Play Store includes the free BBC iPlayer app. This can be installed on your tablet as described on pages 33-36. Tap the icon shown on the right to open the BBC iPlayer as shown below.

The row of icons on the upper right above enable you to switch between TV and radio, then to choose a channel. Tap the three dot menu shown on the right to display the above menu, which gives the options to watch or listen to live TV and radio. Otherwise go back and watch or listen to programs from the previous week, as shown below.

Android Games

The Google Play Store contains lots of free or inexpensive games in various categories, as shown below.

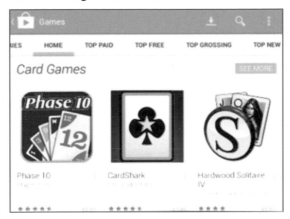

Games are installed as apps on your Apps and Home Screens, as discussed on pages 33-36. To launch a game, tap its icon, as shown on the right.

Robbery Bob

You may wish to group all your games into one or more folders, as discussed on page 40. Tap the resulting circular folder icon to open the folder and give it a name. For quick access, the folder icon can be placed on the Favorites Tray by sliding it into a gap created by sliding away another app, as discussed on page 37. In the example below, a games folder has been placed third from the left on the Favorites Tray.

Streaming versus Downloading

Media such as photos, videos, movies, eBooks, etc., are held as *files* on the network computers of companies such as Google, Amazon, YouTube, Spotify and Netflix. Movie and video files are very large and used to take a long time to transfer over the Internet. Now, with fast broadband Internet, it's more feasible to make a copy of videos, etc., on your Android tablet.

However, movie, video and music files that you buy or rent from the Play Store or Kindle Store are not automatically saved locally on the internal storage of a tablet. They remain in the clouds on the Internet and you must be online to enjoy them.

Streaming

A streamed media file is *temporarily* transmitted to your Android tablet over the Internet and you access it in *real time*. A copy is *not saved* on the tablet. You need to be connected to the Internet to access this file. A *buffer* may be used to temporarily store "chunks" of the video, etc., to guard against interruptions in the streaming process. You will only be able to access the streamed media when you are online.

When a file is *not saved* on your Android tablet you will see this angled-pin icon on the music, movie, or eBook cover in My Library.

Downloading

A copy of a media file is transferred over the Internet and **saved** on the internal storage of the tablet. You can access this eBook, video, movie, etc., at any time in the future, without being connected to the Internet. Downloaded files are needed to use media in Aeroplane mode or where there is no Wi-Fi. Use the menu option **Keep on device** to make sure files are saved on the internal storage of the tablet, as discussed earlier.

Files downloaded and saved on your Android tablet for later viewing offline display a vertical pin icon as shown on the right and on page 70.

Browsing the Web

Introduction

The Android tablet gives us access to millions of Web pages, containing the latest information on any subject you care to think of. Much of this information is of the highest quality, from respected academic, scientific and professional sources.

The Chrome Web browser is a Google product, like the Android operating system itself. Chrome enables you to search millions of Web pages quickly and easily and displays the results in an attractive and readable format. The Google search engine is the world's leading Web search program on all platforms – tablet, laptop and desktop computers. So it's not surprising that an Android tablet is an ideal tool for browsing the Internet to find information. This activity alone justifies the purchase of an Android tablet, not to mention its many other functions such as news, social networking and entertainment, discussed later in this book.

Some of the main functions of Google Chrome are:

- To search for and display information after entering or speaking *keywords* into the Google search engine.
- To access Web pages after entering an *address*, such as **www.babanibooks.com**, into the browser.
- To move between Web pages by tapping *links* or *hyperlinks* on a Web page and move forwards and backwards between Web pages.
- To *bookmark* Web pages for revisiting at a later time.

Launching Google Chrome

To launch Google Chrome, tap its icon on the Apps screen or on the Favorites Tray, shown below.

The **Welcome to Google Chrome** screen opens, as shown below. Tap **Take a tour** to view several pages of notes to help you get started.

The search bar across the top of the screen is the place to start your Web browsing activities. Here you enter either the address of a Web site or *keywords* which should pinpoint the subject you are interested in.

Entering the Address of a Web Site

Every Web site has a unique address, known as its *URL*, or *Uniform Resource Locator*. A typical Web address is:

www.babanibooks.com

Type the URL into the search bar, as shown below and tap the **Go** key on the on-screen keyboard.

For a complicated address you may need to enter the URL in full. However, in practice you'll often find you don't need to be too pedantic; simply entering **babanibooks**, for example, will lead you to the required Web site. If you've visited a site before, it may appear in a list of suggested Web sites which pops up to save you typing the full address.

Instead of typing the URL, as discussed above, you might prefer to tap the microphone icon shown on the right, then speak the Web address.

After entering the address of the Web site into the search bar and pressing **Go**, the Web site's Home Page should quickly open on the screen, as shown in the extract below.

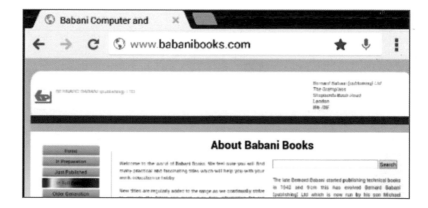

The Keyword Search

This is used to find out about a particular subject rather than visiting a Web site whose address you know, as discussed on the previous page. The Web seems to contain pages covering every conceivable subject in the universe. For example, suppose you were interested in the history of England and Scotland and wanted to find out about the Border Reivers, who were at the centre of the Border's turbulent past. Simply enter **border reivers** into the Chrome search bar, as shown below. (There's no need to use capital letters when entering search criteria — **Border Reivers** and **border reivers** produce the same results).

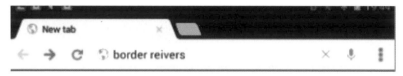

After tapping the **Go** key on the on-screen keyboard, a list of Google search results is displayed, as shown below.

Only the top search result is shown above but a search often yields millions of results. Google places the most significant results near the top of the list. Some results may be irrelevant to a particular search. For example, historians studying the Border Reivers may not be particularly interested in the Web site of the Border Reivers Rambling Club which might appear in the results.

The blue heading on a search result represents a *link* to a Web page containing the keywords, Border Reivers in this example. Tap a link to have a look at the Web site.

Try typing a few diverse keywords into Google Chrome and see how easy it is to find good information on virtually any subject. Here's a few to get you started:

halebop	histamine	entrevaux
making elderberry wine	samuel johnson	thatching a roof
florence nightingale	hadron collider	shearing a sheep

Surfing the Net

On the Web page above, words highlighted in blue are *links*. Tap the links to open further Web pages. Each new page will probably have further links to open a succession of Web pages.

The Internet is surely the world's largest and most up-to-date encyclopaedia covering almost every known subject, no matter how bizarre. For example, type any DIY task, such as **mending a puncture** and numerous Web sites offer helpful advice, often including step-by-step videos.

Previously Visited Pages

As you move between Web pages, you may wish to briefly revisit a page. The back and forward buttons shown on the right and below allow you to quickly move between recently visited pages. Tapping the circular arrow button on the right and below reloads the latest version of a Web page. (For speed, the Chrome browser may load an earlier version of a Web page).

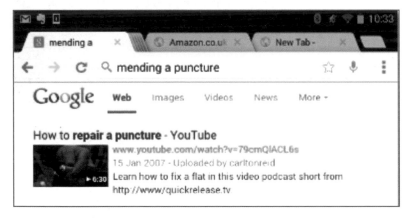

As you move forward or back between Web pages, the keywords from each search, such as **shearing a sheep**, are displayed on the tab at the top left of the screen, as shown below.

Tabbed Browsing

When you do a search in Google Chrome and then proceed to surf the Web, as described earlier, there may be only one tab displaying the current Web page, as described at the bottom of the previous page. However, Chrome allows you to open each Web page in a tab of their own, so that all the tabs are visible along the top of the screen, as shown in the example below.

This makes it easy to move straight to a particular Web page, rather than moving through them all one at a time using the backwards and forwards buttons. Tap a tab to open that Web page. With a large number of Web pages open, the tabs may be stacked on top of each other and can be moved around by sliding or gently swiping left or right.

Opening a Web Page in Its Own New Tab

Tap the **New tab** icon shown on the right and below.

A **New tab** appears, as shown above on the right, with the search bar ready for you to enter your search criteria by typing or speaking. After carrying out the search and selecting a Web page from the list of results, this page appears on its own tab. The search criteria, in this case **green woodpecker**, appear on the top of the tab, as shown below.

Using the Google App

In the previous examples, Google Chrome was opened by tapping its icon on the Favorites Tray. You can also launch Chrome after tapping the Google icon shown on the right, on the Apps screen. Then enter the search criteria, such as **honey buzzard sightings** in this example, in the Google search bar, as shown below.

Tap on a link in the search results to open a Web page you want to look at. The Web page opens in Google Chrome, in a new tab of its own, **Honey Buzzard...**, in this example, as shown below.

To switch to another Web page from a previous search, simply tap its tab, such as **mending a puncture**, partly shown above.

Closing a Tab

Close a tab by tapping the cross, as shown on the right below.

Bookmarking a Web Page

A series of *bookmarks* can be created to enable you to quickly return to your favourite Web pages at any time. With the required Web page open on the screen, tap the star-shaped bookmark icon as shown on the right and on the right of the search bar below.

The **Add Bookmark** window opens, allowing you to name the bookmark or accept the name provided by default. Tap **Save** to add the Web page to the **Mobile Bookmarks** page. To view the bookmarks, tap the three dot menu icon shown on the right and then tap **Bookmarks** on the drop-down menu.

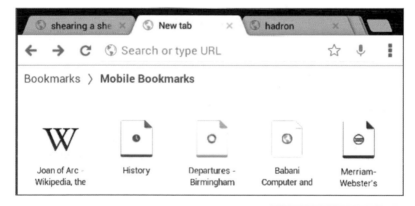

To open one of the bookmarked Web pages, tap its icon on the **Bookmarks** page, as shown above. Press and hold a bookmark icon to display the menu shown on the right, including options to edit and delete a bookmark or add a bookmark to your Home Screen.

Open in new tab

Open in Incognito tab

Edit bookmark

Delete bookmark

Add to Home screen

Displaying Your Browsing History

Google Chrome keeps a record, in chronological order, of all the Web pages you've recently visited. Surprisingly there isn't a button to display the History feature. However it can easily be displayed by typing **chrome://history/** into the search bar.

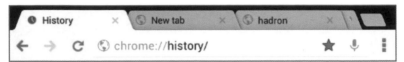

When you tap **Go**, your **History** list is displayed, as shown below.

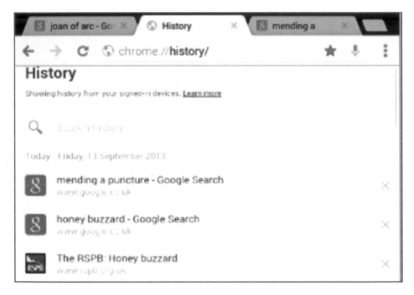

To save time when opening your History, instead of entering **chrome://history/** into the search bar, create a bookmark, as shown on the right. Creating a bookmark is described on page 83.

History

There are options on the History screen to **CLEAR BROWSING DATA** and **Search history**.

Communication and Social Networking

Introduction

This chapter describes the various ways an Android tablet can be used to communicate electronically. Some of the main apps used for these activities are:

Gmail

Google e-mail used by businesses, friends and families to send messages, documents and photos all over the world.

Skype

Free worldwide *voice* and *video* calls between computers.

Facebook

The most popular *social networking* Web site. Enter your personal *profile* and *timeline* and make *online friends* with people having similar backgrounds and interests.

Twitter

Another very popular social networking site, based on short text messages (*140 characters maximum*) which can be read by anyone who chooses to follow the originator, who may be a celebrity, company or a member of the public.

LinkedIn

This is a social network used by professionals for developing their careers and exploring business opportunities with people working in similar fields.

Electronic Mail

Gmail is Google's electronic mail service. It's currently the most popular, ahead of other well-known services such as Microsoft's Hotmail and Outlook.com and Yahoo! Mail. Gmail is powerful yet easy to use and very good at filtering out "spam", the unsolicited junk mail or advertising that can waste a lot of your time.

Gmail is used for creating, sending and receiving text messages over the Internet, as an alternative to sending letters by the traditional post. *Replies* can easily be sent to the original sender of a message you've received and, if necessary, to all other recipients of the original message. An e-mail can be *forwarded* to anyone else you think may be interested.

You can maintain an *address book* for all your contacts and *import* into it files of contacts from other e-mail services.

An e-mail message can include photos and documents, known as *attachments,* "clipped" to the message and sent with it.

Gmail is a Web-based e-mail service, so you can access your electronic correspondence from anywhere in the world. All you need is a connection to the Internet and your Gmail username and password, as discussed on page 22. If someone has already used your chosen e-mail address, just add some numbers, such as **stellaaustin86@gmail.com**, to create a unique address.

There are two e-mail apps on the Android Apps screen. The yellow **Email** app, shown on the right, is used for accessing any of your other e-mail accounts, such as Hotmail or Outlook.com.

Gmail is opened by tapping its icon on the Apps screen, as shown on the right. When you first start using Gmail, an almost blank screen appears with just the words **No conversations** in the middle. Once you've been using Gmail for a while, there'll be plenty of "conversations", i.e. your messages and the corresponding replies.

Creating a Message

Tap the **Compose** icon shown on the top right of the screen, as shown on the right and below.

The **Compose** screen opens, as shown below. Enter the main recipient's e-mail address in the **To** bar. Tapping **+CC/BCC** shown on the right below opens two new lines for recipients who will receive either **Carbon Copies** or **Blind Carbon Copies**. The latter don't know who else has received a copy.

Adding an Attachment

Tap the icon shown on the right and on the previous page. You are then given a choice of locations from which to select the photo, document or some other type of file which you wish to attach to the message. This might be a document saved in My Drive

(discussed shortly) or a picture in the Gallery, for example. Tap the required photo, etc., and the attachments should appear on the bottom of the e-mail, as shown on the previous page. The attachments in this example are the swan photo and a PDF document called **Riviera.pdf**.

Sending an E-mail

When all the text has been entered and any attachments added, tap the **SEND** button on the bar across the top of the screen.

Receiving an E-mail

The e-mail will be available for reading by the recipient almost immediately, or as soon as they open their *Inbox*.

The paper clip icon on the right and above indicates that an attachment has been sent. Tap anywhere on the message header above to open the complete message.

Tap the small photo to open it fully on the screen. To open an attached document, tap its name, as shown on the right. You are presented with a choice of several apps with which to open the document.

Skype

This is a service which allows you to make free *voice* and *video* calls all over the world. Calls between two computers are absolutely free. If you use your tablet to call a mobile phone or landline there is a charge, for which you need a Skype account with some credit in it.

Hundreds of millions of people use Skype to make voice and video calls. You can also send photographs and instant text messages or make and send a video. Android tablets are generally fully equipped for Skype, with a front-facing webcam and built in microphone and speakers. If you also have a rear-facing camera, this can be used to show views of your surroundings during a video call. The Skype app in the Google Play Store is free and can be installed as described in Chapter 3.

Start Skype by tapping its icon on the Apps screen, as shown on the right. Then sign in using an existing Skype username and password or a Microsoft account. Alternatively, if necessary, create a new Skype account. When you sign in, contacts from your address book are displayed, as shown below.

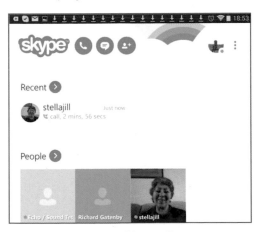

The Opening Skype Screen

Making a Skype Call

Any contacts currently online are displayed with a green dot, as shown on the right and at the bottom of the previous page.

Tap the name or thumbnail of a contact who is currently online. The following icons are available when making a Skype call:

 Start a voice only call

 Start a video call

 Record and then send a video

When you call a contact, their photo and name appear on the screen. The functions of the icons are listed on the next page.

Making a Skype call

Receiving a Skype Call

When someone "Skypes" you, the tablet will emit a distinctive ring and the caller's name appears on the screen. Tap the green phone icon shown on the left below to answer the call.

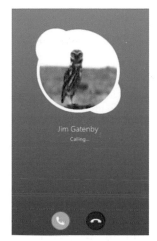

Receiving a call   Answering a call

Shown below are the main icons used when answering calls:

    Answer a video or voice call

    Switch video on or off

    Switch microphone on or off

   Show dialling pad and messages

   End or reject a call

Facebook

This Web site started off in America, as a way for students to introduce themselves and make friends with other students. Now Facebook is the biggest social network, with over a billion users all over the world. To join Facebook, you must be aged over 13 years and have a valid e-mail address. You can access Facebook using the Android Facebook app, installed from the Play Store, as discussed in Chapter 3. Or you can open Google Chrome and enter **www.facebook.com** in the address bar. Either way you will need to *sign up* for a new Facebook account and in future *sign in* with your e-mail address and password.

First you create your own *Profile* in the form of a *Timeline*, as shown on the lower right. This can include personal details such as your schools, employers and hobbies and interests. This information is used by Facebook to provide lists of people who have similar interests or backgrounds to yourself. The list also includes people who are in your e-mail address book. You then send invitations to anyone you want to be your Facebook *friend*. Anyone who accepts will be able to exchange news, information, photos and videos with you.

The term *friends* on Facebook may include close personal friends and family but it might also include people you don't really know. Care should be taken when making friends on Facebook, especially if you've posted your contact details.

The Android Facebook App

Facebook Security and Privacy

The *audience selector* shown on the right appears against the items of personal information in your profile. Tapping the audience selector icon displays a drop-down menu, as shown on the right, enabling you to set the level of privacy for each item, ranging from **Public** to **Only me**. **Public** means *everyone* can see the information, including people you don't know.

Status Updates

These are used to post your latest information and news and usually consist of a short text message and probably one or more photos. Tap **Status** on the top left of the Facebook app screen to open the **Write Post** window shown below. Then enter the text of your post, replacing **What's on your mind?** shown below.

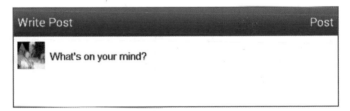

Tap the camera icon at the bottom left of the screen to insert a photo from the internal storage of the tablet.

Finally tap **Post**, shown on the right and above and your friends will receive the update in their *News Feed*.

Twitter

Like Facebook, Twitter is a social networking Web site used by hundreds of millions of people. There is a free app for Twitter in the Google Play Store which can be installed, as discussed in Chapter 3. You can also use the Web version of Twitter by entering **www.twitter.com** into Google Chrome. Signing up to Twitter is free. Once signed up you can either use your e-mail address and password to sign in or you can enter your Twitter username such as **@jimsmith**. Some of the main features of Twitter are:

- Twitter is a Web site used for posting text messages, known as *tweets*, of up to 140 characters in length.

- You can include a 160 character *personal profile* on your Twitter page.

- Photographs can be posted with a tweet.

- Twitter is based on people *following*, i.e. reading the tweets of other people, such as celebrities, politicians and companies marketing their products or services.

- You can follow anyone you like, but you can't choose who follows you. If you have no followers, anything you post on Twitter will remain unread. You could encourage your friends and family to follow you and each other on Twitter, to share your latest news.

- *Hashtags*, such as *#climatechange*, for example, make it simple for other people to find all the tweets on a particular subject. The hashtag is included within a tweet. Tapping the hashtag displays all the tweets on that subject, which might be a campaign or a debate.

- If you like a tweet, it can be *retweeted* to all of your followers, together with comments of your own.

- You can send *replies* to a tweet.

Sending a Tweet

Tap the quill icon shown on the right and on the **Home** screen in the screenshot at the bottom of this page. The following screen opens displaying the words **What's happening?** Replace these with your own message.

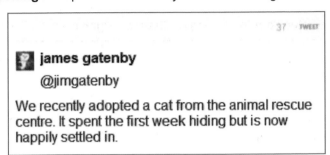

The camera icon at the bottom of the screen is used to take a photo using the camera on the back of the tablet. The icon on the right below is used to browse for photos already stored on the tablet. These photos can then be included in the tweet.

When the tweet is finished, tap **TWEET** shown in the top right of the tweet creation box at the top of this page. Your followers will see your tweet in their Home screen, as shown below.

Responding to a Tweet

If the reader taps a tweet, the following toolbar is displayed.

These icons enable you to respond to a tweet in various ways. Reading from left to right, they are:

Reply, **Retweet**, mark as **Favorite** and **Share** with other people.

Viewing Photographs

If a tweet includes a photo, the reader of the tweet sees a blue link embedded in the text, such as **pic.twitter.com/n8fROHKbyD** shown below. This link is automatically created by Twitter.

Tap the blue link shown above to open the photo on the screen.

Google Drive
and Google Docs

Google Drive

This app brings all the advantages of *cloud computing* to the Android tablet. Suppose you use several computers at different times, such as your tablet and perhaps a laptop and desktop machine. In the past, if you produced a document on one machine you would need to use one of the following methods to transfer it to another computer to carry on working.

- Transfer the files using a removable storage medium, such as a flash drive or CD, etc.
- E-mail the files to yourself as attachments.
- Copy the files across a home network. This requires both computers to be up and running simultaneously.

Using Google Drive, a file or document you save on one machine is automatically *synced* (*synchronised*) to all your other machines, via the clouds. The Google Drive app is free from the Play Store, as discussed on page 33. Google drive is then opened by tapping its icon on the apps screen, as shown on the right.

Drive

You can also download and install the free Google Drive application on laptop and desktop computers, as discussed shortly.

A Google Drive folder is created on each computer on which you install Google Drive. New and edited files saved in a Drive folder are synced to the Drive folders on all your other computers, such as the Android tablet. Google Drive has the following advantages:

- If you always save your files to the Drive folder, all your computers always have the latest editions.

- Your files are professionally managed on Google's server computers "in the clouds". However, if you delete a file from Google Drive, it may no longer be accessible to any of your computers. So I always back up important files to a hard drive, flash drive, etc.

- If you log on with your Gmail password, you can access your files from anywhere in the world.

- Colleagues and friends can collaborate, editing the same document on different machines.

Putting a Google Drive Folder on a Laptop or Desktop

Log on to **www.google.co.uk** on the laptop or desktop machine. Then select the **Apps** icon on the top right of the screen, shown here on the right. From the drop-down window which appears, select the **Drive** icon, shown on the right, to open the window shown below. Then click **Download Google Drive for PC** as shown on the blue button on the left below.

Drive

Google Docs

Once you've installed Google Drive you immediately have access to Google Docs, which is free *web-based software* and includes word processing and spreadsheeet apps. So this software will also be available on any computer with Google Drive installed, after you've signed in with your Gmail username and password.

Although the word processor and spreadsheet software in Google Drive may not be as fully featured as Microsoft Word or Excel, they are quite adequate for most purposes. As mentioned elsewhere, if you want to write a 300 page thesis or typeset a book (such as this one), you'd probably want to use a desktop publishing application on a laptop or desktop computer. As discussed in the next chapter, you can connect a keyboard, mouse and an *HDMI* monitor to turn your Android into a laptop/ desktop replacement machine.

Creating a New Document

Tap the Drive icon on the Apps screen, shown on the right. The **My Drive** screen opens with the following menu bar across the bottom.

Tap the **+ Create** icon, shown above, to open the **Create** window shown on the next page, to start work on a new document.

Scan launches the camera on the tablet allowing you to scan a document and **Upload** is used to send a copy to the Google Drive cloud storage.

Google Drive provides 15 GB of free storage in the clouds, for your files such as photos and documents, etc.

Word Processing Using Google Docs

The **Create** window opens, as shown below, allowing you to create a new word processing document or a spreadsheet. You can also create a new folder within the Drive folder.

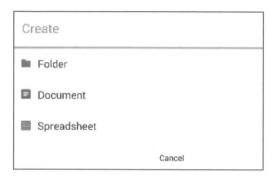

Selecting **Documen**t above opens a window into which you type a title for a new word processing document, before tapping **OK**. The file is created and a blank word processing screen opens, ready for you to start typing the text, as shown below.

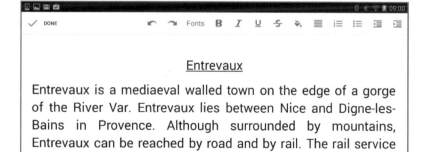

Landscape mode gives a better view of the word processing menu bar at the top of the screen, as shown above, especially on a 7 inch Android tablet.

As shown along the menu bar at the top of the word processing screenshot on page 100, all the main tools are present, such as undo, redo, bold, italic, underline, justification and different font sizes and styles. You can also apply bullets and numbering and text in various colours. Tap a word twice to select or highlight it ready for formatting or editing.

When you've finished entering and editing the text, tap **DONE** in the top left-hand corner and the document is saved automatically in the clouds.

Synchronisation Between Computers

The document is synced to your other computers and you can open it on them as soon as you sign into Gmail and open the Drive folder. The Entrevaux note created on my Nexus 7, is shown below, synced to my laptop PC computer. It also syncs to our desktop PCs and iPads with Google Drive installed.

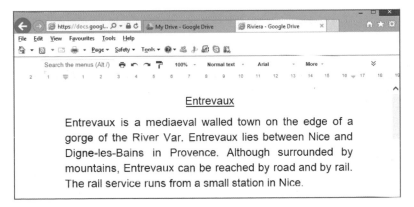

Free Word Processing Apps

The Play Store includes the popular *Writer* from James McMinn, while *Kingsoft Office* includes both word processing and spreadsheet apps. *Evernote* is very popular for keeping notes, making lists and handling photos.

Using the Google Docs Spreadsheet

Tap the **+** icon, shown below, to open a new document, as shown below.

Then select **Spreadsheet** from the **Create** menu, as shown on page 100. A blank spreadsheet opens ready for you to start entering the data, as shown below.

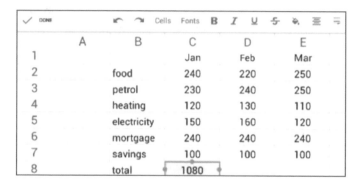

As mentioned on page 100, It's probably more convenient to hold a 7-inch Android tablet in landscape mode, as shown above. If necessary, in order to display landscape view, swipe down from the top right of the screen and make sure **AUTO ROTATE** appears in the Quick Settings panel, not **ROTATION LOCKED**, as discussed on page 49.

This enables you to see all of the icons on the menu bar across the top of the screen, without having to scroll horizontally. Tap to select a cell, such as **C8**, highlighted in blue above. Then use the keyboard to enter or edit data, using the bar at the bottom of the screen, shown below displaying a formula. Tap **abc** to enter letters or tap **123** to enter numbers.

abc   123   =sum(C2:C7)

As shown on the previous page, the spreadsheet app has the normal text formatting tools, such as undo, redo, bold, italic, underline, etc., and text in various fonts, sizes and colours. Columns or rows can be selected for editing by tapping at the top of a column or at the extreme left of a row. Tap **Done** at the top left of the screen to save the spreadsheet in the clouds.

Managing Your Google Docs

The word processing and spreadsheet docs that you create are saved in the clouds as files on a Google server computer. The files are listed on the **My Drive** page on the Android tablet, when you first sign into **Gmail** and launch **Drive**. To open a particular file, tap its thumbnail, as shown below.

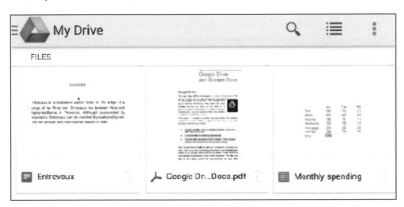

As shown above, **My Drive** in this example displays the thumbnails for the **Entrevaux** document and a **Monthly spending** spreadsheet. In the centre is a thumbnail for this chapter, which was created on a PC computer in PDF format and dropped into the Drive folder on the PC. The chapter then synced automatically from the PC to my Nexus 7 via the clouds.

Files such as photos and documents listed in Google Drive on an Android tablet can also be listed in Google Drive on laptop and desktop computers and iPads.

Press and hold a thumbnail for a file in **My Drive**, as shown on the previous page and you are presented with the following menu, including options to **Remove**, **Rename** and **Print** the file.

Vence.JPG

Send

Move to...

Keep on this device

Open with

Send link

Download a copy

Rename

Print

Remove

Keep on this device saves a copy of the file on the Internal storage of the Android tablet, so it can be accessed when you are not connected to the Internet. Otherwise the file may only exist in the clouds for viewing online, i.e. over the Internet.

For entering a lot of text or numbers, you can use a separate physical keyboard, as mentioned in Chapter 9. Alternatively, tap the microphone icon on the on-screen keyboard and *speak* the data.

Google Cloud Print

This is an app which allows on Android tablet to print documents on paper. Google state that you can use Cloud Print to print from anywhere across the Web to any printer.

If the Cloud Print icon doesn't appear on your Apps screen, it can be downloaded free from the Play Store, as described on page 33.

If you already have a *cloud ready* (Wi-Fi) printer which connects to the Web without being attached to a computer, this shouldn't need any setting up at all. Google provide lists of cloud ready printers in the Cloud Print feature.

A printer which is not cloud ready (i.e. not a Wi-Fi printer), is referred to as a *classic* printer.

The classic printer must be connected by a cable to a laptop or desktop computer **on a home network** and with Google Chrome installed. Open Google Chrome and make sure you are signed in with your Gmail address and password. This Gmail account will need to be used each time you use Cloud Print.

Open the Chrome menu by tapping or clicking the icon shown on the right and in context on the screen below.

From the menu select **Settings** and then scroll down the screen and at the bottom select **Show advanced settings**. Scroll down the next screen and under **Google Cloud Print** select **Add printers** and then select the printer you wish to use. You should now see a message saying you're ready to start using Cloud Print with the current Google Account.

There's also an option to **Manage your printers** as shown below. In this example I have set up a Brother DCP-195C classic printer, connected by a USB cable to a desktop computer.

Printing a Document Using Google Cloud Print

With the document displayed as a thumbnail in **My Drive** on the Android, as shown on page 103, press and hold the thumbnail. Then select **Print**, tap the required printer, set the number of copies, etc., and tap the **Print** button, as shown below, top right.

HP ePrint

This is a cloud printing service developed by Hewlett-Packard, for use with tablet computers, smartphones and laptops. A free HP ePrint app is available in the Play Store. The system requires an ePrint (Wi-Fi capable) printer registered to the HP ePrint Center, which assigns a unique e-mail address to the printer.

The document to be printed is attached to an e-mail sent to the e-mail address of the ePrinter. Documents can be printed in many of the well-known file formats, such as MS Word, PowerPoint, JPEG, PDF and HTML, etc.

Managing Your Android

Introduction

A document, image, photograph or video clip, etc., saved on a computer storage medium, is known as a *file*. There are many different *file formats*, depending on the app or program which has created the file. Some common file formats include *JPEG (Joint Photographic Experts Group)* used for photos and images and *PDF (Portable Display Format)* used for text documents. Files saved in these formats can be opened and viewed on most computers, including Android tablets. Less common formats may not be compatible with the Android, although there may be an app in the Play Store which can be used to open the file.

You may often need to transfer files between an Android tablet and other computers and storage devices. Some methods for transferring files are as follows:

- Connect an OTG (On The Go) cable to the Micro USB port on the Android. This can be used to connect USB devices such as a card reader, flash drive, etc.

- Use a laptop or desktop computer to manage the Android tablet's files via a USB cable.

- Use a cloud storage system such as Google Drive or *Dropbox*.

- Use the Micro SD card slot available on many tablets and smartphones. Manage the files on the Micro SD card with an app such as ES File Explorer.

Google Drive was discussed in the last chapter. The other methods listed above are discussed in the rest of this chapter.

Useful Accessories

The following may be helpful when transferring files between an Android tablet and other devices such as a laptop or desktop PC or Apple computer. You will also need the Android battery charger cable to connect the tablet to another computer.

OTG Cable

This connects the Micro USB port on an Android to a full-size USB female port, allowing various USB devices such as an SD card reader, flash drive, mouse, keyboard and camera to be connected.

The OTG cable

USB Flash Drive

Also known as a *memory stick*, this can be connected to the OTG cable for the transfer of files to and from the Android tablet.

USB flash drive

USB Card Reader

These can take SD cards such as those from a camera, for importing photos to an Android tablet. It can also be used by the Android for saving files. Laptop computers and printers often have a built-in card reader.

USB SD card reader

Micro SD Adaptor

Some Android tablets have a Micro SD slot, allowing a card to be inserted. Files saved on the Micro SD card in an Android tablet can be transferred to a PC computer after inserting the Micro SD card into the adaptor. The adaptor fits into a slot in an SD card reader, which may be built into a laptop or

Micro SD adaptor and card

desktop PC or printer. Micro SD cards are available up to 64GB.

HDMI Cable

This allows the Micro HDMI port fitted to some Android tablets to be connected to an HDMI monitor, projector or TV, so that photos, videos and documents on the Android can bc vicwcd on a large screen.

SlimPort Adaptor

This allows the Micro USB port on an Android tablet to be connected to an HDMI monitor, projector or TV. A standard HDMI cable is used to connect the SlimPort to the HDMI monitor, projector or TV. The SlimPort adaptor

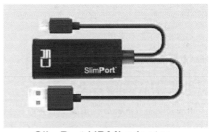

SlimPort HDMI adaptor

includes a USB cable which needs to be connected to a 13-amp plug which has a USB slot, such as the plug used on the Android battery charger. (The SlimPort must be connected to mains power in order to copy the Android display to the large screen).

Expanding an Android Tablet

There are various ways to convert an Android tablet into a replacement for a laptop or desktop computer. As mentioned on page 109, there are cables and Adaptors which allow a tablet to be connected to an HDMI monitor, TV or projector.

The OTG cable shown on page 108 can be used to connect a *USB multi-port hub*, as shown on the right, to which you can attach several devices such as a USB mouse and keyboard. Or you can insert a *USB wireless dongle* into the OTG cable and use this to power a *wireless keyboard* and *mouse*.

Bluetooth

Android tablets generally have their own built-in, short-range wireless technology, known as *Bluetooth*. This can be used to connect devices such as a keyboard, mouse and printer, for working on long documents, etc. **Bluetooth avoids the need for USB cables or dongles, as mentioned above**.

Pairing Two Bluetooth Devices

To connect a Bluetooth device, such as a keyboard, to an Android tablet, the two devices have to be *paired* as follows. On the Android, swipe down from the top right and from the **Quick Settings** window which appears, as shown on page 49, select **SETTINGS** and make sure **Bluetooth** is **ON**, as shown below and on page 50. Then tap the line **Not visible to other Bluetooth devices**, to change it to **Visible to all Bluetooth devices nearby**, as shown on the next page.

Switch on the device you wish to connect and tap **SEARCH FOR DEVICES**, as shown below. On the Samsung Galaxy tap **Scan**.

Any Bluetooth devices nearby such as the **Mobile Bluetooth keyboard for Nexus 7** are listed, as shown below .

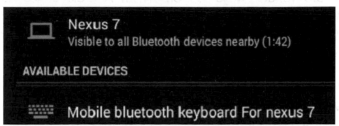

The equivalent list of Bluetooth **Available devices** on a Samsung Galaxy is shown below.

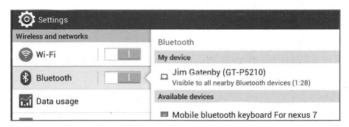

Tap the name of the available Bluetooth device to start the pairing process. If connecting a keyboard you may be asked to enter a given PIN number on one or both devices. In the case of a mobile phone you are asked to check that the same PIN number appears on both phone and tablet. That completes the pairing process and you should then see the paired device listed as shown below. In this example a Bluetooth keyboard for the Nexus 7 has been paired with a Tesco Hudl tablet.

Importing from a Flash Drive or SD Card

This method uses the OTG cable shown on page 108, attached to the Micro USB port on the tablet. The flash drive plugs straight into the standard USB connector on the OTG cable. The SD camera card should be inserted into a USB card reader, as shown on page 108. You need to install a suitable app such as the Nexus Media Importer, available free in the Play Store and installed as described in Chapter 3. Despite its

name I have found the Nexus Media Importer works on Androids in general, such as the Samsung Galaxy Tab 3 and the Tesco Hudl.

After connecting the flash drive or card reader, tap **OK** in response to **Open Nexus Media Importer when this USB device is connected?** A window opens displaying all the folders on your flash drive or SD card. Tap a folder name such as **/DCIM/103-PANA** shown below, to display thumbnails of the photos in the folder. Scroll down, if necessary, to find the required photograph and tap its name. The photograph then appears as shown below.

The **Play** icon, shown on the right and on the previous page, starts a slide show.

The **Copy** icon shown on the right and on the previous page, saves the selected photos in the **Pictures** folder in the internal storage of the tablet.

Tapping the **Share** icon shown on the right allows you to send copies of the photo to numerous destinations such as your e-mail and social networking contacts. You can also send a copy to *Dropbox* or *My Drive*, as shown below, then view it whenever you want to on any computer.

Press and hold a photo, as shown above and a menu appears with various file management options such as **Send** (to destinations such as e-mail and social networking contacts), **Remove**, **Open with** (a particular app or program), **Rename**, **Move to…, Print** and **Make available offline**.

The Nexus File Importer also allows you to import files such as Microsoft Word documents or Excel Spreadsheets which have been created on a PC computer. Free apps are available from the Play Store which allow you to open different types of files for viewing on the Android tablet. Kingsoft Office is a free app for Android which allows you to open and edit Word and Excel files.

Managing an Android Tablet from a PC

The Android tablet doesn't have its own *file manager* for deleting, copying, renaming files, etc. If you have a laptop or desktop computer, you can use it to manage the files on the Android. Connect the tablet to the laptop or desktop PC using the Android USB charging cable. On a Windows PC, the Android, in this example a Nexus 7, appears like a disc drive or flash drive in the file manager, known as File Explorer or Windows Explorer.

The extract on the right shows the **Nexus 7** listed on a laptop computer in the File Explorer in Windows 8.1. Double-clicking the name **Nexus 7** in the list displays the **Internal storage** of the Nexus 7, as if it's another disc drive, here showing **23.9GB** free out of a maximum of **27.5GB**. (The nominal 32GB quoted for the Nexus 7 also includes the operating system).

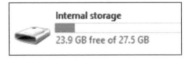

Double-clicking on the **Internal storage** image above displays all the folders on the tablet. Each folder can be opened by double-clicking, such as the **Pictures** folder listed below.

Right-click a file in the file manager window of the PC to open the menu shown on the right. This includes options to use the PC to **Delete**, **Edit**, **Copy** and **Rename** files on the tablet. Files can be copied to and from the Android, by dragging and dropping.

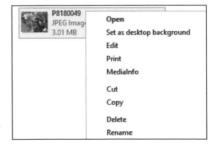

Dropbox

Dropbox is a very popular cloud storage system and an alternative to Google Drive, discussed in Chapter 8. Dropbox has millions of users, both private individuals and businesses. Dropbox initially provides you with 2GB of free storage space on an Internet server, but more is available for a monthly premium.

Your Android tablet has probably already got a Dropbox icon, shown on the right, on the Apps screen. If not you can easily download and install the Dropbox app from the Play Store, as discussed on page 33.

You sign up to Dropbox with an e-mail address and password. If not already installed, download Dropbox to all your computers (tablets, laptop and desktop machines) from the Web site:

www.dropbox.com

The essential features of Dropbox are:

- A Dropbox folder must be placed on all the computers on which you wish to share files.

- You must be signed in with your Dropbox e-mail address and password.

- Save or copy your files to the Dropbox folder.

- Latest copies of files are synced to all your computers.

- Your files can then be accessed on any computer with a Dropbox folder - tablet, laptop, desktop, iPad, etc.

- Important files should still be backed up on local media such as hard drives and flash drives. With an Android this can be done by connecting to a PC as discussed earlier. (Some Androids can also copy files to a Micro SD card as discussed on the next page).

Using a Micro SD Card

Android tablets typically have 16 or 32GB (gigabytes) of internal storage on which to save your photos, music, videos and documents, etc. Laptop and desktop computers often have 500GB or 1000GB (1 Terabyte). For extra local storage, tablets such as the Samsung range and the Tesco Hudl have a slot for a Micro SD card as shown on page 109. The Micro SD adaptor allows the Micro SD card (available up to 64GB) to fit into the full-size SD card slot in a camera or computer.

The Micro SD card is inserted into its slot and clicks into place. From the **Settings** menu select **Storage** and scroll down and tap **Mount SD card**. Then tap **Format SD card**. Formatting prepares a new card or wipes files from a used card.

Files can be imported to Android computers using the Nexus Media Importer. To manage the files on a tablet, you can use a PC, as discussed on page 114. Alternatively, use an Android *file manager* app, such as *ES File Explorer*, available free from the Play Store.

Using ES File Explorer

In ES File Explorer, devices such as Internal Storage (**O**), USB Flash Drive (**UsbDriveA**), and the Micro SD card (**extSdCard**) appear down the left-hand side of the screen. Tap a device, such as the Micro SD card, **extSdCard** and tap to open a folder. Tap and hold a file until the menu shown (in part) below appears,

allowing tasks such as **Cut**, **Copy** and **Delete** files. The **Paste** option allows you to move files between different locations, such as the Micro SD card, internal storage and flash drive.

Cameras on the Android Tablet

Some early Android tablets have one front facing camera. This camera launches automatically when needed in applications such as video calls with Skype. Many of the latest Android tablets have both forward and backward facing cameras, making it easier to take various photos and videos of people and objects.

To take a general photograph, tap the icon shown on the right, on the Apps screen. This opens the backward facing camera. Then another small camera icon allows you to select either a photo or a video. Tap the blue circle at the bottom of the screen to take the photo or video. Images are stored in the **Camera** folder, accessed by tapping the **Gallery** icon shown on the right, on the **Apps** screen. These photos can also be managed after installing a *file manager* app on the Android or by connecting the Android to a PC computer, as discussed on page 114. The photos can be found in the Android **Camera** folder, a sub-folder of the **DCIM** folder, for example:

Internal Storage>DCIM>Camera

Or: **Tablet>DCIM>Camera**

Taking Screenshots on the Android Tablet

You might want to show someone a copy of an interesting screen on the Android. Or you might want to include screenshots in some explanatory notes you are writing, such as this book. With the required screen displayed, simultaneously press the Power/Lock key (shown on page 14) and the Volume down key. You will hear the shutter noise and the screen image shrinks and disappears. The screenshots are saved in the **Screenshot** folder in the **Gallery**, which can be accessed as described above. Using a file manager they can be found in, for example:

Internal Storage>Pictures>Screenshots

File Security
Viruses

These are small, malicious programs or apps designed to damage your files. Most, if not all of the apps you use on an Android tablet are installed from the Play Store. These have been checked for viruses before being accepted into the Play Store. Swipe down from the top right of the screen and select **SETTINGS** then **Security**. The settings below should prevent apps which may contain viruses from being installed.

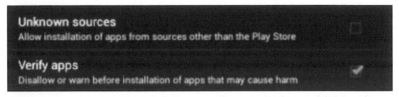

Making Backup Copies

If your only copies of files are in the clouds, you might delete one by mistake. As discussed on page 114, you could connect the Android to a PC computer and copy files to a flash drive attached to the PC, by dragging and dropping or using Copy and Paste. Or install a *file manager* app on the Android tablet.

Setting a Password on the Start Up Screen

You can set a password which must be entered on starting up before the tablet can be used. Select **SETTINGS**, **Security** and **Screenlock**. Select **Password** and enter a suitable one. The following password entry bar will appear on the startup screen.

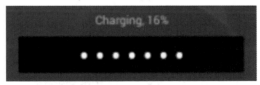

You can also set the screen lock to use **Slide** (or swipe), **Face Unlock** (facial recognition), a drawn **Pattern** or a **PIN** number.

Index